TAX-FREE

How TRIPLE ZERO
Your Future Retirement
While Earning Interest in Two Places at Once

Written By: **Mark J. Orr, CFP® RICP®**
Certified Financial Planner™
Retirement Income Certified Professional®

To learn more about retirement planning, visit
Mark's website and register to join his email list.
www.SmartFinancialPlanning.com

Author of 5 other retirement books, including:
"Get Me to ZERO: 7 Tax Strategies for a TAX-FREE Retirement"
"I Didn't Know Annuities Could Do That!"

3rd Edition—Copyright 2024

All rights are fully reserved, and any infringements of such rights will be vigorously protected/ enforced by all available legal means and financial restitution sought. This book is protected by U.S. and International copyright laws. The reproduction, modification, distribution, transmission, republication, or display of the content in this book is strictly prohibited without prior express written permission from the Author. Any trademarked names in this book are the sole property of their respective companies.

Or our Catapult plans using OPM. Leverage is the source of most great wealth. Responsible leverage is the basis of real estate fortunes; it pours gasoline on business growth and enables acquisitions. Middle America can thank leverage for homeownership, financing college, and buying a car.

However, all the above require monthly repayments of principal and interest. Our one-of-kind loan does not.

Those with "uncommon" incomes can finance a retirement.

Preface	Pg. 3
How TRIPLE ZERO™ Plans Work	Pg. 22
The Powerful "Lock-in and Reset" Mechanism	Pg. 31
Some Client Examples….	Pg. 54
Sequence of Returns Risk	Pg. 74
Accessing Your Cash	Pg. 76
Private Reserve Strategy	Pg. 85
Long-Term Care Benefits (LTC)	Pg. 96
Trade-in the Old for the New?	Pg. 100
Catapult Your TRIPLE ZERO™	Pg. 103
3 Half-Truths and Misconceptions	Pg. 114
TRIPLE ZERO™ Checklist	Pg. 120
Frequently Asked Questions… …Answered	Pg. 123
What's Next?	Pg. 135
About the Author	Pg. 139

Thank you for checking out my book. This book focuses on JUST ONE retirement income strategy for TAX-FREE income in the future. There are others that I use in my financial and proactive tax planning practice, including ROTH contributions and conversions. But the information contained here is too often misunderstood and under-utilized. Let's fix that, OK? Using OPM planning strategies can change your retirement.

Preface

Do you want to pay as little as ZERO income taxes during your retirement? Have more money to spend on YOUR life rather than sending it to the IRS? Do you worry, as I do, about substantially higher future taxes?

Are you really on track to enjoy a huge TAX-FREE income stream when you retire? Do you need to catch up on retirement saving for your desired future lifestyle? Can you envision living a retirement "up" a few notches from what you may be thinking today?

Your future net worth is determined more by "how much" you are saving than by what returns you earn. Catapult plans allow you to save three times more.

Many readers of this book already are (or are on track to be) or have the goal to be a multi-millionaire. Or at least be financially independent. But do you want your millions to be in a 401K that will be taxed at high marginal rates and eventually have Forced Required Minimum Distributions?

Heck no. So, I'll also teach you about our Catapult plan

(my own code name for the strategy) (page 103), which is a very powerful and little-known strategy that allows you to borrow money for a huge TAX-FREE retirement income stream. Yes, you can use 3:1 OPM (Other People's Money) to propel your retirement savings.

The financing? We've done over $4 BILLION of loans for this purpose with NO loan applications, NO credit checks, NO loan documents. NO Personal Guarantees. NO Out-of-Pocket Interest or Principal Payments. NOT Even a Loan Signature. NO Bull! We average 50-100 Catapults a month for folks with at least $150K income.

The catch? The loan funds are contributed to a specially designed, maximum-funded life insurance policy (I personally call it a TRIPLE ZERO™ plan) for the purpose of receiving substantial tax-free retirement income and other benefits.

The Catapult plan is where you contribute 50% to our life insurance policy and a bank loans you the other 50% (at attractive rates) during the 1st five years. Now, your funding is complete. But the bank will loan the full 100% of the premiums for years 6-10. Then, the policy is fully paid up.

Life insurance? You just must hate paying unnecessary taxes more than you don't want great life insurance! Even without financing, TRIPLE ZERO™ plans offer more TAX-FREE benefits than ROTHs (which I also love).

Anyway, we then let the cash value grow and pay off the

bank loan at about year 15 from the cash inside of the policy. All are non-taxable events. Totally tax neutral.

You financed your home to get to live in the home and neighborhood you desired and ought to have—so why not finance a TAX-FREE retirement to enjoy the future lifestyle you crave and deserve? And do so without taking big risks.

I'm one of only a few hundred U.S. financial advisors (out of 600,000+) who have full access to this program! It's not for everybody for sure, but millions of high-earning and millionaire Americans don't even know it exists!

But it all starts with what I call TRIPLE ZERO™ plans that are specially designed life policies. They are the underlying vehicle for this book's content, including Catapult plans (my own name for them) and the PRIVATE RESERVE strategy.

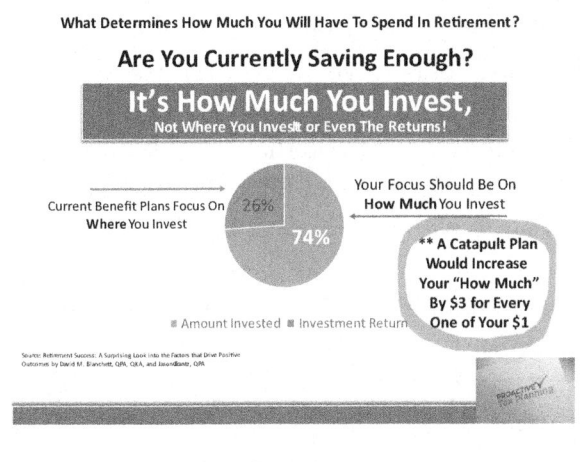

To continue, when the bank loan is paid off, you can now use another strategy to grow even more wealth. I'll teach you another truly unique financial strategy (that I call the PRIVATE RESERVE on page 85—that allows you to have your savings in the life policy – earning compound market-like returns—while simultaneously using those "same" dollars to invest elsewhere. Invest in special opportunities to earn interest or capital gains in a second account.

With or without the Catapult plan, you really CAN have your money earn returns in TWO PLACES at once. But you'll have to think outside of the box and keep an open mind. The basic strategy has been around for decades. But in the last 12 years or so, the inner workings have made the strategy even more flexible and powerful.

You cannot do either strategy with a ROTH IRA/401K, etc. It's against the law. You don't need the Catapult strategy or its sister, the C-Catapult strategy (for Corps) or the Private Reserve, for TRIPLE ZERO™ plans to dramatically improve your financial life. But these plans are at the center of both very powerful strategies.

TRIPLE ZERO™ plans can do that. Just like any ROTH—they can power a TAX-FREE retirement lifestyle. And safely do so with 6%-9%+ average annual returns!

But even without either of these two add-on strategies, you'll learn how TRIPLE ZERO™ plans are genuine RROTH alternatives(or ROTH supplements) on steroids! More benefits now and later, more flexibility, and fewer rules.

SMART, rich people ONLY pay taxes on money that they are going to spend during retirement. You can only do that with tax planning. For many of my clients, the goal is not to die with the most money but to live their desired lifestyle during retirement with the least amount of stress or worry.

So, if planning for a TAX-FREE retirement is something that interests you or learning how your money can earn returns in two places at once, or how to finance your retirement savings using 3:1 OPM, then learning about TRIPLE ZERO™ is the heart of it all. And this book is for you.

Before I get started, let's play a quick game with you. It's called the "Income Game." Below is an image with five guesses. What household income would it take to put you in the top 1% of income? The top 5%? Top 10% and so on?

Is YOUR Income Common... Or Uncommon?

The Income Game

To be in The Top	Household AGI Income Split Point		Percentage of Overall Taxes Paid
1%	?????	?	?
5%	?????	?	?
10%	?????	?	?
25%	?????	?	?
50%	?????	?	?

The point of this game is to have you think about something. If your income is in the top 1%-20%, is your income common... or uncommon? Of course, your income is UNCOMMON! Very uncommon indeed.

Since it's uncommon, should your financial planning be based on what the mass market TV, radio, and magazines are touting for the 75% (which clearly are for the general public or masses), or should your planning be different?

Don't you think someone worth even $5 million is planning differently than you? You could plan the same!

I've been playing this game for years, and the guesses (left column) below are typical. But the important slide is the one on the next page, which shows the actual household income (middle column).

The Income Game

To be in The Top	Household AGI Income Split Point		Percentage of Overall Taxes Paid
1%	$2,000,000	?	?
5%	$750,000	?	?
10%	$300,000	?	?
25%	$100,000	?	?
50%	$65,000	?	?

To be in The Top	Household AGI Income Split Point		Percentage of Overall Taxes Paid
1%	$2,000,000	$548,336	?
5%	$750,000	$220,521	?
10%	$300,000	$152,321	?
25%	$100,000	$85,853	?
50%	$65,000	$42,184	?

But here's the kicker. It's the percentage of overall taxes paid by each group. The top 25% pay over 88% of taxes.

The Income Game

To be in The Top	Household AGI Income Split Point		Percentage of Overall Taxes Paid
1%	$2,000,000	$548,336	42.31%
5%	$750,000	$220,521	62.74%
10%	$300,000	$152,321	73.67%
25%	$100,000	$85,853	88.51%
50%	$65,000	$42,184	97.68%

So again, anyone with a household income in the top 1%-20% in the USA—their income is very UNCOMMON!!

Importantly, who do you think the I.R.S. will tax MOST down the road—the folks with money to tax... or the poor?

Now, I begin most conversations with a prospective

client with this question (and a follow-up). It's a question that helps you put everything in your life into focus and perspective—making your next actions/decisions easier.

Maybe taxes will be on your mind during this next quick discussion. They come up a lot with many of my clients.

Here we go with this sidebar: If we were having this discussion three years from today, and you were looking back over those three years, what has to have happened in your life, both personally and professionally, for you to feel very happy with your progress?

Specifically, what worries do you have now that need to be eliminated, what opportunities need to be captured, and which of your strengths must be maximized?

In fact, what are your three biggest financial worries or fears that you would like to eliminate? Then prioritize them. What are the three biggest opportunities that you need to capture to propel your progress? Then prioritize them. And finally, which 3 of your strengths need to be maximized to the fullest? And again, prioritize them.

In my conversations with clients, once they have verbalized their answers to these critical questions, I can almost always see a newfound clarity on their face.

New confidence in moving forward in the direction

that they "know" will make them feel happier with their progress. Progress towards the things that matter most.

Getting back to retirement and tax planning, in my mind, any and all planning that you do should center on answering those questions. Every financial move and decision should get you closer to feeling happier, safer, satisfied, reassured, and, in fact, gratified over the next three years and beyond. Perhaps reading this book will help you eliminate worries and seize huge opportunities.

Money is just a tool to get what you need and want. ROTHs and traditional IRAs (and 401Ks, etc.) are just a few places to keep your retirement savings. But there's another place too... TRIPLE ZERO™ plans. And as you'll learn they can offer you way more than any ROTH.

I've been a Certified Financial Planner™ for over 23 years, as well as a financial fiduciary (must put their client's interests first). The types of strategies I write about here and in my books are the same ones that I and my own family use to improve our financial futures dramatically.

They may or may not be "right" for you or what you want to pursue yourself, but we've put much of our own money to use in these exact financial strategies. Again, they may only play a small but significant role in your overall financial planning. So just keep an open mind, OK?

So, let's start with explaining TRIPLE ZERO™… and then fill in the details of the Private Reserve and Catapult (and C-Catapult for C-Corps) after that. The more you know, the more possibilities you'll see for yourself.

Financial planning is a focused and straightforward process to meet a stated financial need or desire. It's not a product sale. Financial products/services are only "tools" that professional planners use to satisfy or meet a client's specific goal, objective, or aspiration.

For many people, ROTH conversions and contributions will be all they need to do to enjoy a TAX-FREE income. But not for high earners! They need much more to get to a substantial tax-free retirement. TRIPLE ZERO™ plans can add more benefits, value, and flexibility than ROTHs can (and even executive bonus plans at work), as you'll see.

ROTH contributions are restricted by small $7,000 or $8,000 annual contributions (2024) as well as IRS income limits. ROTH conversions have much more potential "firepower" (no conversion nor income limits), so one can convert $100,000s from traditional IRAs to ROTHs. But taxes will have to be paid at your marginal tax rate.

Renowned IRA expert Ed Slott, CPA, tells us that "Uncle Sam is your partner in traditional IRAs and 401Ks, etc. So how do you get rid of him? The same way you'd get rid of any partner… you'd buy him out" (pay the taxes now).

That's the ROTH conversion. And when appropriate, I use this planning strategy as well, to set my clients up with even more tax-free retirement income.

Paying taxes now is the "price of admission" to the tax-free zone. That way, you can "look poor" on your 1040 tax forms during retirement.

But there are millions of folks like you and I who either can't participate in ROTHs—or need a powerful additional weapon in their arsenal to bring their retirement income taxes as close to ZERO as possible. But to also have enough money in their tax-free accounts to enjoy 30+ years of an extraordinary retirement lifestyle. I'm planning for a truly wonderful tax-free retirement. How about you?

The TRIPLE ZERO™ strategy is that additional powerful weapon to get to or close to our destination—the tax-free retirement zone. As previously written, proper distributions from anything with the name ROTH in it… and life insurance will not show up on your future 1040 income tax forms. There aren't even lines on the 1040 form to fill in for income from these (and other) truly tax-free sources.

So you'll "look poor" on paper since so much of your cash flow to enjoy your retirement years isn't even legally reported, and of course, no taxes are due. Wouldn't it be great to receive $150,000, $300,000, or much more every year and legally not have to pay a dime of income taxes to the IRS or your state? As an "informed" American, you get the option to keep 100% of those tax-free distributions.

Some financial advisors refer to the TRIPLE ZERO™ strategy as a "private" retirement plan.

Now, all cash-value life insurance policies might work, but most life insurance policies are not truly designed to be a ROTH supplement.

Most would make an awful ROTH alternative. The TRIPLE ZERO™ strategy is my Trademarked name for a particular type of life insurance product that is properly designed and fully funded for this purpose.

Let's be clear: in my professional opinion, not just any life insurance policy will work well for this specific use. You need a type of policy (contract) that is specifically designed for this exact purpose (and Catapults use them exclusively).

Term insurance is an affordable way to protect your family from your early death. Most folks don't have nearly enough of it! With no cash value, term life insurance won't work at all for this purpose!

What about whole life insurance? I don't believe that most whole life insurance policies are well-suited for this, either. They do have important guarantees (and you pay dearly for them), but they lack the necessary growth "horsepower" to really do a great job.

A few whole life policies would be OK, but they would likely only provide about 40%-60% of the lifetime tax-free income of the TRIPLE ZERO™ policies that are best suited for this purpose. That's much less future cash flow for your premium dollars.

A traditional Universal Life (UL) policy generally has lower internal costs than whole life policies and market-driven interest rates. Still, UL policies lack the necessary historical growth potential to provide for an increasing income stream for 20-35 years of retirement.

Although Variable Universal Life (VUL) policies do have the growth and accumulation "potential" needed (with multiple mutual fund-like investment choices called "sub-accounts") are also subject to substantial market losses (just like mutual funds). Like 401Ks and brokerage accounts, VUL policies can have big gains... as well as big losses (remember 2000-2002 and 2008?).

Not only that, but the income distribution methods in VULs, ULs, and whole life policies are not designed to provide maximum tax-free retirement cash flow. You need both growth and accumulation potential (without stock market risk) and an attractive and efficient way to enjoy supplemental income distributions during retirement.

Each type of life insurance policy is built differently—although in all cases, the tax-free death benefit is the central focus and feature. The tax-free death benefit of all life insurance policies are significant, and their actual value to your loved ones should never be underestimated.

How do you contribute to a life insurance contract? Well, you can contribute your after-tax dollars just like you would with a ROTH IRA. However, there are NO annual contribution limits (like the $7,000 or $8,000 ROTH limits).

Nor are there any IRS income limits that would prevent anyone from putting huge sums of money into a life policy. Your income can be as high as you can imagine, and you will still be able to fund your life policy. That's what I do.

You can do a "TRIPLE ZERO conversion." If you are under 59½, you can take advantage of the 72(t) rules (avoiding the 10% early withdrawal penalty), shift some money from a traditional IRA (pay your income taxes now), and fund your life insurance contract with the rest. That way, you convert money from a tax-postponed account into the "never-taxed" zone (assuming you follow IRS rules).

Cash-value life insurance has been used as a tax-advantaged accumulation vehicle for decades by hundreds of major corporations, successful small business owners, banks, the wealthy, and the "informed."

About 3,800 banks own $140 billion of bank-owned life insurance, including ten major US banks that have over $60 BILLION of their Federal Reserve "Tier 1 capital reserves" requirements were safely invested in this SAME "asset class." If it's good enough for the Federal Reserve, shouldn't it be worthy of your consideration?

It's no gimmick or a passing fad. Now, it can be your turn to take advantage of it. This fully IRS-compliant "cash value" insurance planning tool is a near-perfect family protection, savings, and supplemental retirement planning vehicle. In fact, three Congressional Acts in the 1980s (TAMRA, DEFRA, and TEFRA) codified the rules.

So, let's take a closer look at TRIPLE ZERO™—one of the best tax-free alternative retirement savings vehicles that Wall Street doesn't want you to learn about. It's a prudent retirement strategy that offers "peace of mind" and a tremendous number of other valuable current "living" benefits that you don't have to die… to enjoy!

TRIPLE ZERO™ life policies have these three "ZERO" characteristics plus much more: 1) ZERO income taxation 2) ZERO stock market risk and 3) ZERO I.R.S. contribution or income limits.

Proper withdrawals (following the IRS rules) from a life insurance policy are not subject to income taxes. We'll discuss this much deeper further in this book.

There are no IRS contribution limits, unlike a ROTH IRA and ROTH 401k (and similar work-based retirement savings plans). One could fund a life policy with $100,000s a year. And unlike ROTH IRAs, life insurance does not come with IRS income limits—Congress not choosing who can and can't own one!

We'll talk about ZERO market risk and how that works in a moment, but first off, what do I mean by a TRIPLE ZERO™ life policy? Again, TRIPLE ZERO™ is my own name to describe a certain type of life insurance policy. It's a planning tool that has so many advantages over traditional IRAs, 401Ks, and brokerage accounts.

It's a specific type of a "tax-advantaged life insurance contract" (TALIC) called Indexed Universal Life. One that can be (and needs to be) specially designed and maximum-funded for the goal of paying as little as ZERO income taxes during your retirement.

Index Universal Life, also known as an IUL, has many "living" advantages over traditional tax-postponed accounts that make it a perfect complement or perhaps an alternative to any ROTH.

Just like any IRA or 401K, your money grows tax-deferred. But like a ROTH, when you take money out of your account correctly—even at any time BEFORE age 59½ too—you can access your money <u>without</u> any income taxes or 10% early penalties.

That's right, even accessing your earnings can be done tax-free according to tax laws on the books since 1913.

And finally, just like the ROTH, when you pass away, your spouse or heirs get all the money income tax-free as well. But the death benefit is much larger than the account value. That sounds pretty good, doesn't it?

You get stock market-linked returns with NO downside risk to your principal (or even your past year's gains) due to stock market drops. No matter how much the stock market plummets, your worst annual return credited to your account is <u>ZERO</u>.

You avoid all market losses entirely. Now, that's a pretty safe, predictable, and some would say "stress-free" plan. Plus, you get the flexibility and security that allows you to comfortably stay invested in the market—even through all of the economic recessions and bear markets you will likely face over the next 30-50+ years.

What if you knew that you would never have another losing year again, and even your past gains would always be "protected" from future market losses? Do you think that you could stay invested in an asset that historically gave you 70%-85% of the market's returns, which over time beats inflation... and yet still sleep well at night?

According to Forbes Magazine on April 27, 2017, "Many people do not view life insurance as an essential and vital part of a retirement income plan. They see life insurance primarily as a way to protect families from the early loss of a breadwinner during the working years."

However, life insurance has the potential to be so much more if properly utilized in a comprehensive retirement income plan." They can offer a lifetime of access, control, and flexibility. It is an important "asset class" of its own.

In that same Forbes article, "Russ DeLibero, CFP® ChFC® CLU® who also holds a Ph.D. in Financial and Retirement Planning, notes "that there are tremendous uses of life insurance in a retirement income plan because of the preferential tax treatment that life insurance receives. Both before and during retirement."

According to Dr. DeLibero, "When properly structured, life insurance can provide tax-deferred growth, tax-free cash flow, and a tax-free death benefit. The tax-preferential treatment provided to life insurance allows an individual to have greater flexibility over which dollars to use (before or) during retirement, and depending on the type of life insurance, it can also provide a non-correlated asset to the portfolio, providing additional diversification."

That's right; life insurance can be a separate, non-correlated asset class to stocks, bonds, real estate, etc.

Steve Jobs (co-founder of Apple) repeated this statement often, "People do not know what they want... until you show it to them." And I'm here to show it to you!

Again, you don't even have to like life insurance. You just must like it more than you do paying future income taxes to the IRS and your state. Here's a quote from the Huffington Post website in 2013. All of the bullet points below will be fully discussed later in the pages that follow.

"Life insurance is a very powerful yet fairly essential financial planning tool that has been used to solve myriads of financial planning goals for decades. Some of the many uses of a properly structured and funded life policy include (words in parenthesis are mine):
- Providing supplemental retirement income for corporate executives, everyday employees (and the self-employed).
- Creating a self-completing retirement plan (the tax-free death benefit to protect your loved ones from your early death).
- Avoiding the threat of higher income taxes in the future. ($34+ TRILLION of federal debt)
- Addressing estate tax issues at death & paying off debts.
- Guaranteeing what you want to happen financially in life will happen, whether or not you are alive to see it happen.
- Becoming your own bank and making more efficient purchasing (financing) decisions. Providing (nearly unfettered) access to your funds that may be earmarked

for retirement purposes (unlike IRAs, 40Ks, etc.)
- Having multiple investments with the same dollars. (Your own Private Reserve—explained later)
- Paying for a college education without being disqualified from financial aid (529 plans can cause disqualification).
- Addressing long-term care (LTC) needs later in life.
- Creating a (truly) tax-free income stream at retirement."

So, don't get hung up on the words "life insurance"—or you will really miss out! Over $2.7 BILLION of cash went into <u>newly purchased</u> IUL policies from people just like you in 2022 alone. And the word is just starting to get out about these robust "private tax-free retirement" plans.

How TRIPLE ZERO™ Plans Work

Let's talk about this powerful financial tool that offers a death benefit, the safety of principal, ample liquidity, very good potential returns plus ROTH-like tax benefits and more. And even more importantly, there are no IRS contribution or income limits.

First of all, when we are using an IUL to accumulate cash, we do the EXACT OPPOSITE of what you'd do if you were buying life insurance only for the death benefit.

So instead of looking for the largest death benefit for the smallest premium, we buy the LEAST initial amount of life insurance the IRS allows and stuff as much cash into that policy as quickly as the IRS code 7702 will permit. That's the important key to accumulating tax-free cash.

There are various forms and slight differences between how the various IUL policies from different insurers work, but most work in the following or a similar way. The interest credited to your policy is "TIED" to a stock index—usually the S&P 500, over 12 months. Sometimes, other market indexes and/or time periods are used in addition to the basic formula, depending upon the IUL policy.

Now let's be clear: even though the interest credited to your contract is TIED to how well the S&P 500 index performs (excluding dividends), your money is NEVER actually invested in the stock market, which is why you cannot ever lose money due to market downturns.

My overall financial planning process always revolves around being fully defensive and prepared for the bad times—yet ready and opportunistic to profit in the good times. Each investment should have a defined "job description." An IUL does both very well, and it fully handles the goal of tax-free retirement planning.

Let me give a general description of how IULs work and how they avoid stock market risk. As the name "Indexed" Universal Life implies, the interest "return" is determined by an index or indexes such as the S&P 500, Dow, Russell 2000, or the Barclays Bond index.

Many insurance carriers are even coming out with their own proprietary "blended" indexes to offer you more choices and more consistent returns in all types of economic markets. These proprietary indexes are the latest innovation in TRIPLE ZERO™ plans.

Anyway, once you pay your premium (monthly, quarterly, or usually annually) to the insurance company, the company invests those funds into their general account, which is invested in investment-grade bonds.

The insurer could pay you an interest rate as a CD from what it earns on its bond investments minus its overhead, expenses, and profit margin. They call that their "fixed account." Your bank does something very similar; it pays the depositor an interest rate that depends on its loan portfolio interest income minus its overhead, expenses, and profit margin.

Many IULs will offer their policyholders a one-year fixed rate of 3.5% - 4.5% or so (the insurer's fixed account) right now. Way better than most banks but not very appealing for most people saving for retirement.

As the owner of an IUL, you have the right to forego getting that fixed interest rate and have those interest payments buy options on an index(es) such as the S&P 500, NASDAQ, Russell 2000, etc.

By using options, you can participate in the upside of the index when it goes up. But there is a catch – you usually don't get all or even most of the upside in a very good year. Because of the option strategy(s) you choose, you are "limited" in the amount of interest that can be credited to your IUL by a "cap," "spread," or a specific "participation" rate. I'll explain these terms in a moment.

Also, by using options instead of investing your actual principal, you can never get a loss since your funds were never invested in the index. And the worst thing that can happen with the option strategies the insurer uses is that the options expire worthless.

When that happens, no interest is credited to your policy that year. In other words, you get a ZERO return.

When the stock indexes crashed as they did in 2000, 2001, 2002, and 2008, ZERO was your hero! It's much better to get NO return... than to experience a big loss. Your principal and past gains can never go backward due to market losses in an index.

Because of the use of options, when the index goes up, your gain is limited by either a cap, spread, or participation rate. A "**cap**" is the most the interest will credit one year (say 9%-12%), based on 1) the index used, 2) the cost of the options, and 3) the amount the insurance company can spend on the options (which is about equal to the interest they would have paid you in the fixed account. Historically, most indexes in IULs have used caps.

So, with a cap, if the S&P 500 index prices gained 22% as it did in 2017, and your IUL had an 11.5% cap, that's the amount of interest that your IUL would have been credited with that year. Should the index earn 9%, since that is lower than the cap of 11.5%, you would earn the full 9% that year. Caps are best when the actual index returns are relatively low (under 9%-12%) or just under the cap.

A **"participation rate"** means that you would get a certain percentage of the index's gain, such as 60%—with no cap on what you might earn that year. A participation (par) rate can give you the potential for more upside in a BIG gaining year. So, with a par rate of 60%, if the index went up by 30% as in 2013, your policy would be credited with an interest rate of 18% that year. When the index does 8% with a 60% participation rate, your interest credit would be 4.8%. If the index returned -16%, you would be credited with 0% that year. It's better than taking a loss!

Like participation rates, a "spread" also allows for some big potential gains when the index has large gains—with no cap! Think of a "**spread**" as a hurdle. An 8% spread means that you don't get any interest credited unless the index beats that amount (the spread).

But you get ALL of the gains above the spread amount

credited to your policy. Again, if the index repeats 2013 and gains 30% with an 8% spread, your account would be credited with 22% interest. If the index returned 9%, then you would get credited 1%. If the index only did 2%, the 8% spread is larger than the gain, and you would get no (ZERO) interest that year.

Whether an index uses a cap, participation rate, or a spread, in years like 2008, where there was a considerable drop (-37%) in the S&P 500, you get 0%. Many of my IUL clients proudly told me that "ZERO was their HERO"! Their IUL was their best performing asset since almost everything else they owned (stocks, mutual funds, real estate, etc.) went down in value and took years to "get back to even." **The after-tax equivalent yield of 7% in an IUL is 10%-12%.**

It's evident that a ZERO percent return was awesome compared to a -37% loss. The main thing to know is that your account value can never decrease because the stock market goes down. You avoid all market losses. Your 401K can't do that. Even money in a ROTH, if it is invested directly in the stock market, will decline in value.

Again, with a "cap," in years where the S&P 500 does well, your contract will be credited with an interest rate that is limited to a cap—say between 10%-12% a year. So, if the actual raw S&P 500 index goes up by 20% (excluding dividends), the interest credited to your policy is limited by your policy's cap, perhaps 11%.

But whether your IUL uses a cap, par rate, or spread (some offer all of them), unlike the actual S&P 500 index, your annual gains are always locked in and can never be lost by future market drops—ever. I'll write about "lock-in and reset" in a moment. This is huge and is one reason the TRIPLE ZERO™ plan is so stress-free.

Yes, those annual gains become principal and are never again subject to market risk, nor can they ever be lost when the market goes down the next time—which it will. Some people may see caps as a negative. But, if you never have to make up for bear market losses and your past gains are protected forever, it's really tough to beat these products' long-term performance of over 6.5% - 9%+ gross average after-tax annual gains when you consider the valuable downside protection. Those good returns come with no stock market risk. No losses due to negative markets.

In fact, a policy with a 0% floor and an 11% CAP would have equaled or beat the raw S&P 500 index that had NO caps on its gains, nor limits on its annual losses, in quite a few single "15-year rolling investment periods" from the depression years through 2019—with less risk and stress.

How does "indexing" work? The insurance company uses only the interest they earn from your premiums (they do NOT use any part of your premium/principal) to buy call options on the S&P 500 index (or whatever the index(es) are being used). If the index goes down, the options expire worthless, and you get no return (0%) that year. But then the advantage of the index "reset" comes in. Wait for a few pages to learn more about this valuable feature.

You can take the fixed interest (say 4%) or look for more upside with the indexing. The insurance company doesn't care if you take the fixed interest or use that money to buy the call options. They are totally agnostic to your choice.

Indexing gives you more potential. If the index goes up, the call options make a profit, and your account is credited with the entire gain on the call options (up to the cap, participation rate, or over the spread).

Neither you nor the insurance company can earn any more profit on the call options. Your principal never has market risk, and you enjoy the potential to make double-digit gains each year when the index does well. The worst thing that can happen is getting a ZERO % return in a bad year. You never go backward due to the market. You never have to regain lost principle due to market losses.

Your absolute worst years are 0%, and your best years are up to 11%-20%+ (averaging about 6.5% - 9%+ per year over time). When you combine the insurance company using only the interest they earn from your principal to buy risk-free options with the annual "reset" (described below); you get attractive potential account growth without market risk. That's what I do with my IULs.

"Hope" is not a retirement plan—it's just another four-letter word. It's certainly not a plan that you can rely upon. A properly designed IUL from a great insurer (AM Best "A+" rated or better) along with ROTHs and other tax-free strategies, can provide the basis for a great retirement. Pay the IRS less in retirement and gain a better lifestyle.

Would you sleep better at night knowing your account can never lose money when the market goes down, and yet you can enjoy (and keep) up to double-digit gains in years when the market goes up? Would never having a negative year again and protecting all of your past account gains be a good bet for you?

Well, with no market risk, one must expect to give up some market upside. There is no perfect place to save. But here's another advantage of the IUL.

The Powerful "Lock-In and Reset" Mechanism

Another essential advantage to understanding TRIPLE ZERO™ plans is the "reset" mechanism. The power of the annual reset mechanism is that you get to actually grow your account when the market REBOUNDS after the big stock market drops.

Meanwhile, mutual fund and stock investors are hoping, waiting, and praying just to get back to breakeven—back to before the crash happened.

Is your portfolio ready for the next market drop or economic recession? Will you be profiting during the eventual market rebound like IUL owners always do?

As I update this book on Dec 10, 2023, the S&P 500 is still in "bear market" territory—a 20% drop from the recent highs (Jan. 2021). There may be more to come. We'll see.

The graphic below is an example comparing the IUL to a low-cost S&P 500 index mutual fund (excluding fees, expenses, and dividends in both cases).

In the next hypothetical chart, the IUL and S&P 500 index are shown. Both have a $200,000 starting value. Let's see how the Lock and Reset works and how they compare in "equity market rebounds" after a market loss. Let's say you had $200,000 each in your IUL and the S&P 500 index mutual fund on May 14th when the S&P 500 index was at 2500.

The first year, the price of the index gained +12% (to 2800), so both products got that same dollar gain (since the IUL cap was 12%). Both accounts rose to $224,000 that year (excluding fees, expenses, and dividends).

The Powerful Advantage of Locking in Annual Gains

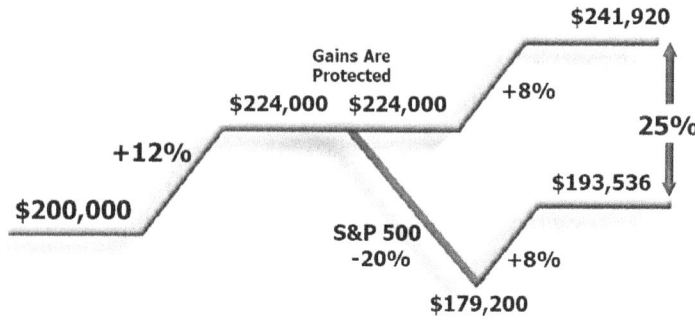

$48,384 positive difference due to the annual lock-in and reset

By May of the 2nd year, the index went down by -20% to 2240. As you'll see, if your IUL policy credited the "floor" of 0%, your contract account would still be worth $224,000 even though the market crashed. Your past gains were locked in. ZERO was your hero. There were no market losses to ever need to regain. In golf terms, you get a mulligan every time the market plummets.

Meanwhile, your S&P 500 index mutual fund would have gone down 20% in value along with the index with an ending value of $179,200. That's a loss of over $44,000 in the mutual fund. The IUL avoids all market losses.

In the IUL, we calculate the potential gain from where

the index ended on May 14th of the year before (2240). During the following year, the index rose +8% to 2419. The gain of the first year was locked in, and the $224,000 became principal in the IUL. But the mutual fund still must grow back to $224,000 before it gets back to break even.

In the mutual fund, an +8% gain (from the index value of 2240 to 2419) on $179,200 value brings that account up to $193,536 at years-end. That's still over $48,000 less than the IUL. That's not chump change.

Even though the index gain for the IUL is calculated from the same 2240, the 8% index gain adds 8% to the value of the IUL. An 8% gain on $224,000 equals $241,920. That's a 25% larger value than the mutual fund. Of course, the mutual fund does not have a cap (participation rate/spread), slowing its growth in many years as it does in the IUL... but mutual funds can have significant losses, too.

And those losses in the fund must be made up for... before higher account values can be enjoyed. The $193,536 mutual fund will have to grow 40% to catch up to the IUL (assuming the IUL is capped out at 12% in the 4th year—rising to $270,950 (not shown on the graph).

That's a very important factor to consider. Losses must be made up for when you're in the stock market while the IUL keeps moving forward (although subject to a cap, par rate, or spread) and before all policy expenses.

Here's an analogy of a 0% floor and an 11% cap. Would you play blackjack if, when you lost a hand, the worst thing the dealer did was give you back your entire bet without a loss? And when you beat the dealer's hand, you'd win up to 11% of your bet. And that 11% gain would be protected and could never be lost in future hands. If you knew that your chips were never at risk, would you keep playing? Most people would play that game all day long.

And what if those gains would be tax-free when you need supplemental retirement income? That's pretty cool.

Of course, you can get the same protection from loss of principal, if you invest in CDs and fixed annuities... but you generally do not get the potential of earning 10%-12% or more—nor are those gains tax-free (unless they are invested in your ROTH).

You don't need to hit home runs to enjoy a great retirement. Just singles and doubles without any losing years will do the trick—especially with no future income taxes on your gains.

Warren Buffet said, "Unless you can watch your stocks decline by 50% without becoming panic-stricken, you should not be in the stock market." Do you remember how you felt back in 2008? During the quick COVID crash?

If you want to take the stock market risk, that's what the

ROTHs are for (although these investments can be principal protected or have a good bit of risk mitigated depending on where you invest these funds—described in later chapters). The ROTHs give you tax-free income, and if you want more market risk, I would take it in your ROTHs.

The IUL gives you the same tax-free benefits, reasonable rates of return (but not the highest returns in a long, huge bull market), with protection from market losses. That's the risk/reward ratio many folks are looking for.

So let's compare investing in the raw S&P 500 index to a hypothetical IUL policy. If you had $500,000 invested in the S&P 500 index on January 1st, 2000, and you took the actual historical annual returns of that index, including dividends but no fees, your account would only be worth $535,000 on 12/31/2011.

That's just a 1.07%% average gain on your money over those 12 years. Little actual growth, but you'd have "real" losses for over a decade in "inflation-adjusted" terms. Your money would actually buy less stuff. And you likely had a great deal of stress too, with four negative years.

Could that happen again? Another lousy decade in the market? That's what Vanguard Investments had been predicting in late 2021. Ask me. Or how about another prolonged bear market?

However, if you were a 45-year-old healthy male that put the same half-million dollars into an IUL contract on January 1st, 2000, with a death benefit of $3.49 million, your account value... the actual cash value in your contract would have grown to about $657,000 by the end of 2011. And that's EVEN AFTER deducting all of the policy loads, insurance costs, fees, and all other charges.

Despite having capped returns when the stock market did very well, the IUL simply avoided the four years of market losses.

That's a difference of over $122,000 actual dollars in favor of the IUL in a decade of lousy stock market returns. That insurance contract had a ZERO percent floor and a 12% cap. By the way, the S&P index went up by +16% (including dividends) in 2012. Would you rather get the full +16% gain on only $535,000... or get a 12% capped gain on $657,000 in the IUL? Which ending figure will be larger?

Plus, the stock market's future performance can never take those new gains away since they would be locked in and protected from the next recession and/or bear market. That's powerful and helps reduce your retirement worries. Don't you want to consider hedging at least some of your retirement risk along with the risk of rising taxes?

Should you at least explore owning even a small IUL? It's kind of like "buy term and invest the rest" on steroids.

Yes, for those who are Dave Ramsey or Suze Orman fans who tell you to only buy term insurance, they are partially correct. You can and should protect your family with the right amount of term insurance—purely for the death benefit. "Term" is the cheapest way to get the full amount.

Most Americans are woefully underinsured, and their families are going to have to rely on a "gofundme" to live beyond the first 5-7 years after death or dramatically reduce their lifestyle. Most people should have at least 10-20 times their salary in life insurance death benefits, depending on their other assets and circumstances.

TRIPLE ZERO™ plans are more than a death benefit. It's a ROTH alternative with no income or contribution limits with protection from market losses. The money going into the indexes is the "invest the rest." All in the tax-free zone.

Anyway, remember that if he died during that period, his spouse would get $3,469,000 income tax-free compared to the value of his S&P 500 mutual fund. Yes, you do get something for those policy fees and expenses!

I call that an "explosion clause." TRIPLE ZERO™ plans are "self-completing." In other words, if you die prematurely, the 100% tax-free death benefit instantly achieves your future savings goal. So, your beneficiary doesn't have to worry about how they are going to save for retirement, the money will be there.

The statistics say that you'll probably live well into your 80s, but what if you die way before your time? The "what if"... is another significant tax-free benefit of the TRIPLE ZERO™ plan, just in case.

In fact, let's look at what investors call the "lost decade," which was 2000-2009, where there were 4 negative years in the S&P 500 (2000, 2001, 2002, and 2008), while the "cap" method enjoyed the protection of no losses!

By the way, the IUL index with just the 10% cap and the 0% floor earned an actual average return of +4.46% over the same "lost decade" (2000-2009) versus the actual avg. return in the S&P to be -0.95%/year (including dividends)! Now, to be sure, I picked a bad ten years in the market. So, let's take a broader look at the recent 50-year period: 1972 to 2021. Fifty years. Don't forget that 2022 was bad!

We'll compare the S&P 500 Total return (including ALL dividends) to both an IUL with an 11% cap (excluding dividends) and one using an 8% spread. The "Annual Return %" column is the Total Return S&P 500 index (with dividends) and the "Limited Return %" is the IUL (excludes dividends). These are two popular strategies using the S&P index. Most IULs offer other indexes, including proprietary indexes as well.

The chart below on the left side is using the 11% caps and the one on the right shows the IUL with an 8% spread (with no cap). In both charts, the S&P 500 index (including dividends) but no fees had an actual rate of return of +11.1% over the 50 years. That assumes the investor never panicked or sold during the 3-year bear market of 2000-2002 nor panicked in 2008 either!

I'd say that would be pretty unlikely, and the well-respected DALBAR investor studies seem to bear that out. And there are many other indexes and index strategies we can use for even higher annual returns!

The capped IUL had an actual rate of return of +7.51% over that 50-year-time period. It captured 67% of the index's total annual return of 11.1% (S&P 500) without market risk or any stress during recessions/bear markets.

It had more consistent returns than the IUL with a spread and performs better than a spread in a "not-so-great year."

The chart on the right is for a slightly more aggressive index. The index (one of many) in this IUL has an 8% spread which means you get no gain until the S&P index has at least an 8% gain. That's the hurdle. That chart shows the results if you opted for this index every single year.

Now, I would never keep the same index allocation for 50 years. Nor would I normally only use one index. I prefer to diversify into two or more indexes. I'd at least look at changing them every year depending on the markets.

By using the "spread" indexing method, over that 50-year period, it would have had an actual rate of return of +9.18%—capturing 82% of the index's 11.1% total gain. Again, this is with no stock market risk. ZERO is your hero.

In fact, let's look at what investors call the "lost decade," which was 2000-2009, where there were four negative years in the S&P 500 (2000, 2001, 2002, and 2008), while the "cap" method enjoyed the protection of no losses!

By the way, the IUL index with just the 10% cap and the 0% floor earned an actual average return of +4.46% over the same "lost decade" (2000-2009) versus the actual avg. return in the S&P to be -0.95%/year (including dividends)!

In so-so years, the index with the cap did better than the spread. But in very good and great years, the index with the spread beat the capped IUL... but it had a few more lower-earning years due to the spread. That's why I typically diversify the index allocations between various indexing strategies in every TRIPLE ZERO™ plan that I design and manage for my clients.

Check out these two 50-year charts on the next page. Although my wife and I each own an IUL with the "spread," most IULs do not include that option. And the spread is not available in the IULs we use for the Catapult plan. However, it will work great for the PRIVATE RESERVE strategy over time as it takes advantage of great market years.

With 11% Cap

Year	Annual Return %	Limited Return %
1972	18.90	11.00
1973	-14.77	0.00
1974	-26.39	0.00
1975	37.16	11.00
1976	23.57	11.00
1977	-7.42	0.00
1978	6.38	6.38
1979	18.20	11.00
1980	32.27	11.00
1981	-5.01	0.00
1982	21.44	11.00
1983	22.38	11.00
1984	6.10	6.10
1985	31.57	11.00
1986	18.56	11.00
1987	5.10	5.10
1988	16.61	11.00
1989	31.69	11.00
1990	-3.10	0.00
1991	30.47	11.00
1992	7.62	7.62
1993	10.08	10.08
1994	1.32	1.32
1995	37.58	11.00
1996	22.96	11.00
1997	33.36	11.00
1998	28.58	11.00
1999	21.04	11.00
2000	-9.10	0.00
2001	-11.89	0.00
2002	-22.10	0.00
2003	28.69	11.00
2004	10.88	10.88
2005	4.91	4.91
2006	15.79	11.00
2007	5.49	5.49
2008	-37.00	0.00
2009	26.46	11.00
2010	15.06	11.00
2011	2.11	2.11
2012	16.00	11.00
2013	32.39	11.00
2014	13.69	11.00
2015	1.38	1.38
2016	11.96	11.00
2017	21.83	11.00
2018	-4.38	0.00
2019	31.49	11.00
2020	18.40	11.00
2021	28.71	11.00

7.51% Avg

NO Cap – 8% spread

Year	Annual Return %	Limited Return %
1972	18.90	10.90
1973	-14.77	0.00
1974	-26.39	0.00
1975	37.16	29.16
1976	23.57	15.57
1977	-7.42	0.00
1978	6.38	0.00
1979	18.20	10.20
1980	32.27	24.27
1981	-5.01	0.00
1982	21.44	13.44
1983	22.38	14.38
1984	6.10	0.00
1985	31.57	23.57
1986	18.56	10.56
1987	5.10	0.00
1988	16.61	8.61
1989	31.69	23.69
1990	-3.10	0.00
1991	30.47	22.47
1992	7.62	0.00
1993	10.08	2.08
1994	1.32	0.00
1995	37.58	29.58
1996	22.96	14.96
1997	33.36	25.36
1998	28.58	20.58
1999	21.04	13.04
2000	-9.10	0.00
2001	-11.89	0.00
2002	-22.10	0.00
2003	28.69	20.69
2004	10.88	2.88
2005	4.91	0.00
2006	15.79	7.79
2007	5.49	0.00
2008	-37.00	0.00
2009	26.46	18.46
2010	15.06	7.06
2011	2.11	0.00
2012	16.00	8.00
2013	32.39	24.39
2014	13.69	5.69
2015	1.38	0.00
2016	11.96	3.96
2017	21.83	13.83
2018	-4.38	0.00
2019	31.49	23.49
2020	18.40	10.40
2021	28.71	20.71

9.18% Avg

Not shown is a multiplier. One IUL offers one S&P 500 index, which has a 10% spread with no cap. But here's the kicker: you can OPT to pay a 7.5% fee (you can choose this every year, only some years, or never choose it). What do you get for the BIG fee? A multiplier.

Well, whatever that index earns after the fee and spread, they multiply that by 270%. So, if the index netted 14% (after the above) in a policy year, your interest credit would be 37.8% that year (14% x 2.70). And that gain would never be subject to future market losses due to the "lock-in."

Now, that index option is not for the faint of heart, but it would certainly be attractive in a market rebound after a bear market or recession. It's not available in the Catapult. My wife and I each own this IUL as part of our collection.

Most IULs offer other indexes for more diversification.

Here's one that I like in one of my personal IUL policies and how it has done since 2006. This index offers a 145% participation Again, the IUL is a perfect supplement and/or alternative to your ROTH contributions or conversions. Although ROTHs have contribution and/or income limits, not everyone qualifies to get an IUL either. You, your spouse, or someone else with whom you have a legal "insurable interest" needs to be healthy enough to qualify for life insurance. There's a quick medical exam to complete, too. There's NO CAP plus a 15% interest bonus.

Bloomberg US Dynamic Balance II ER Index annual point-to-point with a participation rate (Standard)

17-year historical index performance		
Date	Actual historical performance	Hypothetical historical return
12/31/2005	-0.83%	N/A
12/31/2006	6.12%	11.25%
12/31/2007	2.86%	5.26%
12/31/2008	0.37%	0.67%
12/31/2009	5.81%	10.68%
12/31/2010	8.46%	15.57%
12/31/2011	5.19%	9.54%
12/31/2012	6.92%	12.73%
12/31/2013	8.01%	14.74%
12/31/2014	6.88%	12.67%
12/31/2015	-1.33%	0.00%
12/31/2016	4.93%	9.06%
12/31/2017	14.73%	27.11%
12/31/2018	-0.66%	0.00%
12/31/2019	12.83%	23.61%
12/31/2020	4.45%	8.18%
12/31/2021	4.81%	8.85%

Historical compound average return			
	From	Through	Historical average return
10-year	01/01/2012	12/31/2021	11.39%
15-year	01/01/2007	12/31/2021	10.32%
20-year	N/A	N/A	N/A
25-year	N/A	N/A	N/A

Nowadays, many IULs have interest bonuses. Most are NOT guaranteed, but some do have guaranteed interest bonuses of, say, 15%, which would make the returns in the above charts even greater. Some of these have no extra cost but have lower caps or participation rates.

Again, some IULs allow you to buy more upside for an asset fee. The OPTIONAL fee generally runs from 1%- 8% and buys 40% to 270% bigger gains in the underlying index performance with the multiplier. This fee allows the insurer to buy more options. One of my colleagues had a client actually earn a +151% return from the March 2020 COVID lows to March 2021. That was luck and likely won't happen again. You can read more about this in one of my blogs: www.smartfinancialplanning.com/not-a-fan-of-iuls/

Unfortunately, under the new insurance regulations of Dec. 2020, we cannot illustrate or project the positive effect of multipliers that have a fee. But in good market years, they will definitely boost actual performance and help overcome the "cap" objection, which does limit returns. Although, again, the 0% floor eliminates market losses. And my clients appreciate that feature.

   Most IULs use cap strategies, and some use participation rates or spreads. Some, like the index above, use a combination of two or three. Picking an IUL based only on having the highest cap, lowest spread, etc., may sound good, but it is not the smartest thing to do. There are some other very important components and features to making an IUL a great policy. I'll discuss those later.

   Before we go on, let me make an important point about stock markets. THERE IS NO LAW of ECONOMICS that says they must always go up over time!!

   Below is a chart from YahooFinance.com of Japan's Nikkei 225 index (their S&P 500) from 1989 to 2021. Back then, Japan was the world's 2nd largest economy after the USA. Today, it's number three after the USA and China. It's still a huge economy.

   In 1989, their stock market peaked at nearly 40,000. That was over 34 years ago, and it has never been close to that mark since. At the end of 2021, it was still under 29,000!

Japan's Nikkei 225 stock index 1990-2023

This is an extreme (but factual) example of stock markets not going up over long periods of time. Investors in Japan have never even gotten close to becoming whole. Imagine new retirees in 1989 trying to spend their dwindling savings over the rest of their lives. In about 2003, the Nikkei 225 index finally hit about 9,000 at its low—a -75% drop over about 14 years. It ended in 2023 at about 33,000! It's still 8% off its all-time high in 1989—34 years later.

   I'm certainly not proposing anything like what happened in Japan will happen in the USA. We are the greatest country in the world. But this chart does prove that unlike our normal regular bear markets and subsequent recoveries, there is no law of economics that promises markets must ever recover… or even recover on any particular timetable. I just thought that was worth bringing up. OK, let's continue.

Traditional tax-postponed IRAs, 401Ks, etc., are simply "tax wrappers." And the same thing goes with anything with the name "ROTH" in it. They are both tax-wrappers—not investments. They just describe how that investment is going to be taxed at distribution, and perhaps some other rules like deductibility and RMDs, etc.

Both traditional IRAs and ROTHs can be invested in just about anything—CDs at your bank, stocks, bonds, mutual funds, annuities, etc. (although neither a traditional IRA nor ROTH can be invested in a life insurance policy).

So, besides explaining the tax and other ramifications of IRAs and ROTHs, I don't need to explain what a CD or a mutual fund is here. But that's not true for life insurance—whether it's a whole life policy, variable UL, or an IUL.

Many folks know at least something about ROTHs. But most readers don't know much about or have pre-conceived myths about life insurance. But with having NO CONTRIBUTION limits, using properly structured/funded life insurance can help you attain a tax-free retirement.

Hopefully, you've learned a little about how interest in your IUL is credited to the policy—potential double-digit returns when the market does well and no losses due to bear markets and recessions. So, in addition to adding another potential source of tax-free income to your plan, you can also avoid stock market risk in the IUL.

One financial planning software I use in my personal practice is Circle of Wealth®. The founder and CEO of that company is a brilliant man named Don Blanton. He has come up with a pretty concise explanation of life insurance called the "10-minute lesson" (a snapshot of it below). I'll take less time than that here.

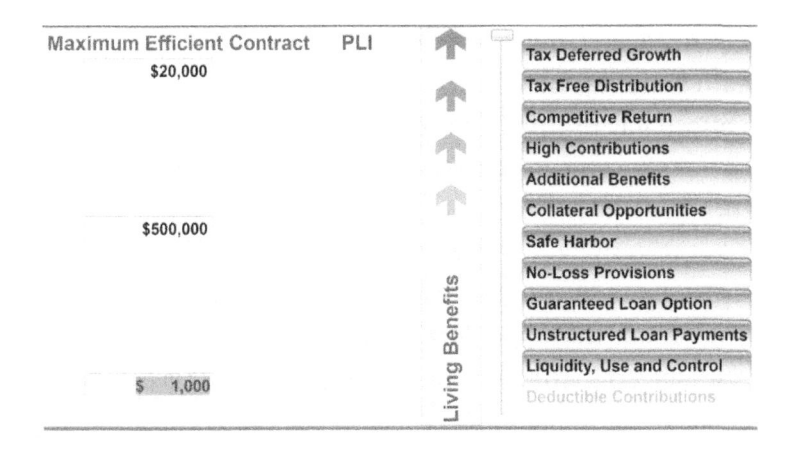

Maximum Efficient Contract	PLI		
$20,000			Tax Deferred Growth
			Tax Free Distribution
			Competitive Return
			High Contributions
			Additional Benefits
			Collateral Opportunities
$500,000			Safe Harbor
			No-Loss Provisions
		Living Benefits	Guaranteed Loan Option
			Unstructured Loan Payments
			Liquidity, Use and Control
$ 1,000			Deductible Contributions

Why would anybody pay $20,000 annually for a $500,000 death benefit when their sex, age, and health would allow them to buy the same amount of death benefit for just $1,000? Obviously, the buyer must be getting a lot more than just a death benefit.

You've probably already guessed that the $1,000 premium is for a term insurance policy. Maybe one that fixes the premium for 10-30 years. Who determines and sets the price (premium) for that term life policy? The insurance company does. Not you, and not the IRS.

And what does the policyholder get with a term policy? Usually, only a death benefit should he/she die during the term. It's like renting versus buying a home. It's less expensive because relatively few people (only 1-2%) actually die while their term life insurance is in force.

Am I suggesting that buying term insurance is a mistake? Heck no! Again, most people don't have nearly enough death benefit protection, and "term" is a wonderful way to affordably protect your loved ones. But a term policy will not give you any cash flow during or even before retirement.

Now, who do you think sets the $20,000 maximum premium for the same death benefit in a permanent life insurance policy (PLI) for the same person in this example? The insurance companies?

Heck No! It's the federal government that sets the maximum. Yup, it's the IRS that determines the max premium amount one can put in that $500,000 policy in this example (based on the sex, age, and health of the insured).

In the 1980s TAMRA (Technical and Miscellaneous Revenue Act) and DEFRA set the minimum death benefit according to a complicated formula that allows for a policy's favorable tax treatment. They boil down to what's called the MEC limits (Modified Endowment Contract) which would make withdrawals from your policy... taxable. Nothing wrong with a MEC policy in and of itself, but we want to avoid a MEC policy as a supplemental tax-free retirement strategy.

Whether the policy is a MEC or a non-MEC, the death benefit is always tax-free (except in some pretty rare pension situations).

Of course, if you'd like to put more than a $20,000 premium in (for the TAX-FREE strategy), you'd just have to buy a bigger death benefit. So there really is no practical annual premium limit to get you the supplemental tax-free income you're looking for.

The MEC limits don't determine the amount of premium you can pour into a policy, just the minimum amount of death benefit that amount of premium must purchase (depending upon your sex, age, and health). MEC limits also apply to how fast you can put money into your policy.

To avoid a MEC in an IUL (a quick rule of thumb), you generally can't fund it any quicker than 3 years and a day (if you're under age 50) and 4 years and a day if you're older than that.

For example, my buddy out in Denver has a wealthy client putting $500,000 a year into his minimum death benefit policy. I can't recall if he's paying that premium for 4 or 5 years, and then they will stop making premiums payments. There are some 1,000+ people putting in at least $1 million a year into life policies. Some fortunate few, $10 million/year or more.

Without really getting in the technical weeds on this, the big difference between a non-MEC policy and a MEC policy is how they are funded and how any distributions out of the policy will be treated for taxation. With the MEC, any earnings taken out of the policy will be taxable and a 10% penalty would also apply if the owner were under age 59½—(sounds like a non-deductible IRA to me). So, for tax-free planning—we definitely want to avoid a MEC.

Now, if the government is regulating the most premium you can put into the policy—what does that say about it? It says that it must be good—and "good" for you in relation to your income taxes. The premium limits for tax-free retirement cash flow fall right below the MEC line.

Don Blanton calls the MEC line—a "Maximum Efficient Contract." The difference between taxable... and tax-free. You don't want a MEC for tax-free access.

A non-MEC policy is a Tax-Advantaged Life Insurance Contract (TALIC). That's what you want for another source of non-taxable cash flow in retirement. By "maximum funding" your policy with the "minimum death benefit" allowed by the IRS—it brings you right below the MEC line.

On the right side of the chart above, you can see a list of many desirable benefits one would like in a savings vehicle. A non-MEC policy can provide them all—except for the one listed at the bottom— "Deductible Contributions."

You don't get that one. Darn! Oh well. Nothing's perfect.

The more you contribute to your non-MEC policy, the greater the degree of those listed benefits you'll enjoy. By funding your policy with less money, you get fewer benefits. Also, by fully funding your contract, you reduce the internal costs of the policy (as a percentage of your cash value) over your lifetime and increase your returns.

With the wealth-building goal of TRIPLE ZERO™, you want to focus less on the size of the death benefit (which the MEC line will determine for you) and more on the amounts you feel comfortable contributing to this portion of your tax-free retirement plan.

Depending upon your sex, age, and health, you can contribute a similar amount to a ROTH ($550 a month) up to $100,000 or much more a year. You can fund your TRIPLE ZERO™ policy for 20-30 years or longer—or complete paying for it in just four or five years (and anything in between). The policy funding design can be very flexible at inception... or along the way.

Now your stockbroker, advisor, or know-it-all neighbor

will say that cash-value life insurance policies have expensive loads, fees, and charges, which is very true... ESPECIALLY IF it is NOT structured properly to accumulate and grow your cash with the minimum non-MEC death benefit allowed by the IRS rules.

Your policy needs to be properly designed by someone who really knows what they are doing and who is only looking out for your best interests. If it's not, then don't buy it for tax-free planning!

Over your lifetime, IUL policy expenses will ONLY cost you about .9% or less a year for the Death Benefit. That's about what many equity mutual funds charge you to chronically "underperform" the stock market.

Historically, a fully funded IUL contract should have an actual cash-on-cash, TAX-FREE internal rate of return (IRR) of between 6%-7%+ over the long-term—even after ALL insurance loads, fees, and charges are deducted.

You would need to consistently earn a pre-tax rate of about 8%-12% a year to equal that tax-free rate of return—depending upon your personal federal, state, and local income tax bracket.

I'll show some client examples in a few moments. All without market risk.

And since we are all going to pass away someday, at least the tax-free death benefit gives you something of VALUE for your .9% or so of long-term average annual policy expenses. Most actively managed "buy and hold" mutual funds can't honestly say they add any value over indexing, but they still charge you each and every quarter of every single year. They get paid their fee in the awful years... or the good ones.

Have you watched the 60 Minutes and various YouTube videos about high 401K fees— (many 401K plans can cost you up to 1.5% - 3% each year), which can actually "rob" you of $100,000s in total lost retirement income? That's in addition to taking on all stock market risks, having virtually no access to your money, and causing your Social Security to be taxed, as well as paying those postponed taxes on your future income at unknown rates/brackets.

Now, if you are thinking about putting money in an IUL (or any cash-value life insurance policy) and take most every penny out of it within 5-8 years (basically surrendering the contract), then this isn't the right financial vehicle for you. Don't do it. These policies are built for the long run, as you'll see in a moment. Remember the tortoise and the hare. Steady wins the retirement tax-free cash flow race.

But if you want steady long-term performance, safety, and complete flexibility (plus good tax-free cash flow down the road), a properly designed and funded IUL is a great supplement and/or alternative to the ROTH. Don't forget that economic recessions happen about every seven years, and with an IUL's lock and reset, you'll never have to recover from another one again.

Combined with any ROTH strategy, the TRIPLE ZERO™ plan can add tremendous lifetime value for you. No other financial vehicle can match the benefits of no market risk, double-digit potential returns when the market does well, the annual reset, <u>access</u> to your cash pre-59½ without penalty or tax, and tax-free distributions.

And the death benefit is a huge "bonus" for your loved ones if you happen to die too young. But, the real benefit is for YOU... if you <u>live</u> a long life, as you'll see next!

Some Client Examples...

Tim is one of my Texas clients. He's a 47-year-old who is worried about future increases in income tax rates and the potential of reduced Social Security benefits for all but the poor. You don't need to be a higher earner.

Right now, he can only comfortably afford to contribute $600 a month to his IUL in addition to the $6000 annual ROTH contribution, and he plans on doing so (but is in no way committed to doing so) for 19 years—until age 66.

The minimum non-MEC death benefit for his age and health is just $100,000. A 30-year term policy would cost him a bit less than $50 a month. But Tim was looking for "invisible" retirement cash flow to supplement his ROTH — not a death benefit. He already has a $1 million 20-year term policy to protect his wife (plus coverage at work).

Suppose Tim makes all of the planned contributions, and we average just 6.6% gross annual rates of return (not the historical crediting rate of over 8% as it did over the last 15 years in this policy, so I'm being conservative). In that case, he could start drawing over $20,000 per year of TAX-FREE income from his policy at age 67... for the rest of his life. I think it will likely be more.

If Tim passed away at age 90, he could have enjoyed over $440,000 of tax-free distributions from his IUL — after ALL policy fees, costs, and expenses. At age 90, there would be an additional $167,000 of the tax-free death benefit paid out to his family (assuming he died at that age). Of course, should Tim still be alive, the income continues till age 120.

Now, that may not sound like a lot of income, but remember, it took him a whole 19 years to contribute a total of only $137,000 to the policy. (Obviously not a Catapult). If Tim had put in the same $137,000 in fewer years, his results would have been even better. Again, that's after ALL insurance policy costs, expenses, and fees (which are primarily front-loaded in the first 10-15 years).

At age 90, his cumulative net internal rate of return (IRR) on his 19 years of paid premiums was 6.85% (after all fees and expenses). And that 6.85% IRR was after-tax since this cash flow does not show up on any tax returns (just like cash flow from a ROTH). So, depending upon future tax rates, it can be equivalent to a 9.5% - 12% pre-tax return.

And since this is life insurance, his spouse or kids will eventually get a net death benefit of over $167,000 tax-free (at age 90) on top of those policy distributions. The total "living" and death benefit from his $137,000 contributions could be $607,000 TAX-FREE or more.

During the early years, his policy expenses are high, but they don't stay high forever. At age 75, for example, he still has about $189,000 of cash value left in his policy, and the total policy expenses for that year are $539. That is a total policy cost of just .003% during that year. After decades, the IUL expenses have become much less of an issue and it does pay a death benefit. TRIPLE ZERO™ is a long-term income program—not a 100-yard dash.

All of his income projections above are based on an average of 6% gross interest credited to his policy from the various index methods that are available to him in this particular policy. As I mentioned, the historical returns over the last 15 years were just over 8%, so I am conservative in my forward projections for his gross interest earned. Tim will likely do much better than those projections.

I have another 52-year-old builder in California who transferred about $94,000 from an older life policy (via a 1035 tax-free exchange) and is planning to make 13 years of $75,000 annual contributions into his newest IUL for a total contribution of $1,069,000. This is his 4th IUL policy with me. He earns too much money to contribute to a ROTH and does not have a ROTH 401K at work. Like me, the IUL is his best tax-free alternative.

I'll call him Dan. His non-MEC minimum death benefit is over $1,100,000, and like the gentleman described above, it will increase with each premium payment for maximum growth of his cash value. It's the same with a Catapult. Unless you are just going to make premium payments into your IUL for 4-5 years, having an increasing death benefit helps maximize your cash accumulation.

Anyway, using the same 6.6% projected average annual returns (when the historical returns have been over 8%), at age 67, the cash value should be over $1,700,000. Again, this isn't even a Catapult. Just a self-financed IUL, using after-tax dollars, that he could use as a Private Reserve.

But in the 17th year, his policy expenses are just $2,466 that year. That's a total expense of only .0022% that year. Less than 2/10ths of a percent of his $1,498,000 cash value. Cheaper than Vanguard!

At age 67, Dan should enjoy more than $140,000+ a year

in tax-free cash flow from this TRIPLE ZERO™ policy alone. At that point, Dan's death benefit will have grown to about $1.9 million. So, either Dan himself or someone he cares about will be well taken care of.

Although it's his largest IUL, he will have "invisible" distributions (legally not shown to the IRS on the 1040 tax form) from his other three IULs, too. Remember that Dan doesn't qualify for a ROTH. And none of these huge cash flows will make his Social Security taxable!

At age 90, Dan's cumulative after-tax IRR will have grown to 6.75%. By age 90, he'll already have received over $3.25 million in tax-free cash flow from this TRIPLE ZERO™ policy. Should he pass away that year, the net death benefit to his loved ones and/or charity will be $1.1 million.

Although, if Dan is still alive beyond age 90, the growing tax-free distributions will still be paid every year. Not a bad alternative to a ROTH, is it? Pay the IRS less. Keep more and have a better life.

The IRS contribution limits won't allow you to contribute $75,000 a year into a ROTH 401K—even if one was available to him at work. So how else is Dan going to save enough for the retirement lifestyle that he envisions and avoid annoying annual 1099s from a taxable account?

I truly believe that his income will actually be higher than what I projected (and his IRRs, too). Even a +.25% increase in his projected +6.6% average returns will make a big improvement since all of the policy expenses have already been fully deducted from the cash value.

And there is another reason that the income will likely be higher in all my client examples shared here—it's called "loan arbitrage," which I'll fully explain later.

In any case, there's nowhere else to put that amount of money that will be tax-advantaged for the rest of his life. Not only that, but he has unfettered access to his cash surrender value at any time (we'll discuss the "private reserve" strategy in a later chapter), no market risk, lock-in and reset, and a giant death benefit should he get hit by a bus along the way.

Jennifer is a 36-year-old audiologist who is contributing enough money to get the full match into her company ROTH 401K. Then, she decided to add to her retirement savings by putting away $1,000 per month into an IUL until the age of 66 (she loved the idea of the Private Reserve strategy). Savings working in two places at once.

The lowest initial death benefit in her case (per IRS tax regulations) starts out at $261,000. It will grow to over $1.3 million by the time she retires at age 66 from her total of $360,000 in contributions ($12,000 x 30 years) and using 6.6% projected average returns (lower than historical crediting rates).

Like all life insurance, her beneficiary would get a huge death benefit if something awful happened to her—but we "built" this policy for "living" benefits for Jennifer and her family. (Note: she's added a Catapult since this policy).

She can access some of the cash in her policy at any time and for any reason (estimated to be over $448,000 at her age 56)—without any taxes or penalties—even before retirement. A powerful part (the Private Reserve) of the Get Me to ZERO™ strategy!

At her retirement age of 67, she could start taking planned tax-free distributions from her policy of $97,000/year. This income will not cause her Social Security to be taxed nor ever show up on her tax return.

And Jennifer's had no stock market risk nor any market stress along the journey. But let's say she gets hit by lightning at age 86. Over just those 20 years, she would have received over $1,940,000 million in tax-free withdrawals from her IUL, and she would still leave a tax-free net death benefit of $794,000 to her loved ones.

And if she didn't pass away at that age, her $97,000 tax-free annual income would continue for the rest of her life, and she would still leave a substantial death benefit behind. After-tax money "in"—all tax-free money "out."

Here's a teaching moment. I usually like to spend ROTH and IUL money "last" during retirement (though each person's situation and goals are different). In Jennifer's written retirement income plan, I have her delaying taking any money from the IUL for just 5 more years (to age 71). Everything else being equal, that could increase her initial tax-free annual income from her IUL to $140,000 (instead of $97,000). That's over 44% more tax-free annual income.

That's a $43,000 higher tax-free lifetime cash flow by delaying just five years! Of course, she could begin distributions early as well (for a lower annual income).

So why is having supplemental non-taxable income in retirement important? Because taxes will likely be much higher due to our huge and growing government debt, Social Security, Medicare, etc. being a financial mess.

According to an article in the April 1, 2018, edition of Fortune magazine, the federal debt has <u>tripled</u> from 2007, and it will probably double again by 2028 (likely much earlier now since 2022). "To ensure long-term (fiscal) stability, policymakers (Congress) will have to do something that's been almost unthinkable in recent memory—simultaneously cut spending and pump-up revenue" (taxes). (The parentheses are mine).

That's what David Walker (former Comptroller of the USA under Bush and Clinton) has been saying to anyone who will listen since 2010. Getting as much retirement cash flow off the IRS's radar screen as possible is simply smart tax diversification. Anyway...

People under age 59½ who want to convert their traditional IRA to a ROTH but don't have the funds outside of the IRA to pay the income taxes due can use Section 72(t). For these folks, the 72(t) can provide the answer to use some of the IRA money itself to pay the IRS the taxes due and avoid the 10% early withdrawal penalty. It's at least a partial, potential solution (but not perfect).

You may know that a 72(t) cannot be used to fund a ROTH conversion. So, if you want to get more of your traditional IRA savings into the tax-free zone (the Get Me to ZERO™ strategy), the only other genuinely tax-free place to put those funds into is a well-designed and maximum-funded (TALIC) life insurance policy. Do you still hate life insurance? Or do you hate paying taxes more?

Again, under the tax laws, any permanent life policy will work. But in my opinion, the structure and benefits of an excellent IUL contract make it the superior choice. A distant second choice would be one of a couple of select whole-life policies – but you'll sacrifice potential future income.

Steve is a married 46-year-old executive with $430,000 sitting in an old 401K from his previous employer that he wanted to roll over into an IRA (step 1).

He fully understood the benefits of a ROTH conversion but did not want to pay the tax out of his taxable brokerage account. Nor did he want to pay the 10% early withdrawal penalty by using his own IRA money to pay the federal and state income taxes.

He had about $360,000 in a brokerage account, and he was getting nervous about being in the tenth year of a bull market. He's moved $45,000 of his account to a money market fund for any emergencies.

Steve spoke with his CPA about taking advantage of some capital gains in the account—selling some stocks at their highs. You'll never go broke by taking profits.

Again, he wants to keep tax bracket management in mind but not let the "tax tail… wag the dog." It's better to pay taxes than take a big market loss sometimes.

Anyway, he wants to move some $15,000 a year from his brokerage account (net of capital gains taxes) into the TRIPLE ZERO™ plan, too. This will also reduce his 1099s that the I.R.S. will expect him to pay taxes on every year.

Finally, his new job does offer a ROTH 401K, and he is going to max out his contribution and get the full company match. He'll contribute $12,000 to his ROTH 401K and get the full $6,500 match (into the traditional 401K). Like millions of Americans, his income is too high for him to be allowed to contribute to a regular ROTH IRA.

So, calculating his 72(t) amount (based on his age, IRA balance, and the current applicable interest rate), he must take $19,807 out of his IRA and pay the income taxes due (avoiding the 10% penalty) until at least age 59½. However, he plans to continue moving the tax-postponed IRA into the IUL until he retires at age 66 (21 years).

After paying 28% (22% federal and 6% state) taxes, he'll have $14,261 available to pay the IUL premium plus the $15,000 after-tax from his brokerage account for a total of $29,261 premium per year into the IUL.

With the insurance carrier we chose, the minimum initial death benefit was $411,000. His wife Teresa liked the fact that she had some valuable additional financial protection should the worst happen to Steve. They still have 3 kids at home. The death benefit increases each Steve contributes.

Using a conservative 6% average annual gross return from the multiple indexing strategies within the policy, when he is finished funding his IUL, it should have almost $1.24 million of net cash value, and the death benefit will have risen to about $1,650,000—after all policy loads, fees and expenses had been deducted.

Along the way, Steve will have the opportunity to take advantage of $100,000s of his policy's cash value by using the Private Reserve strategy to potentially profit by having his savings working in two places at once (upcoming chapter). You can't do this with any ROTH.

When Steve retires at age 67, he should be able to enjoy $110,000 of annual tax-free cash flow until age 120. I think it will be much more. This would be in addition to tax-free income from his ROTH 401K. None of this income would cause his Social Security income to be taxed, either.

It's unlikely that he'll live beyond age 100, so let's say he passes away at age 92. By then, he will have taken a cumulative $2.75 million out of his IUL policy, and Teresa would still be left with a tax-free death benefit of $760,000 then. That's a combined tax-free benefit of $3.4 million.

Jason is a 62-year-old man who just inherited some money from his mother. After paying some bills, making two ROTH contributions, and planning a very special 30-year anniversary trip to Europe, he wants to put the $150,000 leftover cash into a TRIPLE ZERO™ plan.

He wants to position this money in a place where, unlike a taxable brokerage account, he won't get annual 1099's for interest, dividends, or capital gains. He does not want any more stock market risk than he is already taking in his traditional 401K. He also worries about owning bonds in a rising interest rate environment since he understands that rising interest rates generally cause the value of bonds to go down. And most "fixed" bond income has a hard time keeping up with inflation. And, of course, he worries a lot about rising tax rates—big tax increases!

Jason has had a few health issues in the last eight years, but he's in pretty good health now. Although his doctor says he should lose 20 or 25 lbs.

As I wrote earlier, for someone about age 50 or older that wants to fund his IUL as quickly as possible and still avoid a MEC contract (to keep the tax-free advantages), he can fund the policy at $30,000 a year for five years. Then, his contributions to his policy are complete.

Since this is a short-pay situation (only 4-7 years of contributions), it's usually more efficient for accumulation to have a level death benefit (rather than increasing along with the premium deposits). In Jason's case, the death benefit is just under $289,000.

Again, I used only a 6.6% gross average annual interest crediting rate from a selection of indexes available to him in this policy. Again, I think he'll get closer to the 7.25% over time that most of this policy's indexes have earned.

After all policy fees and expenses, at age 75, Jason would have just under $200,000 in cash value inside of his policy.

Keep in mind that he really wasn't looking for a death benefit. He was more interested in a tax-advantaged place to put some of his inheritance, but the death benefit does have a real value, which reduced his gains over time.

Like Jennifer, the longer Jason leaves the money in the policy, the faster the cash value will continue to grow.

That will start pushing up the cash value to about $505,000 at age 89 and over $1 million at age 100 (and the death benefit will grow as well).

Of course, since he avoided a MEC in order to get tax-free access to his cash at any time, whenever he needs some of that money, he won't have to worry about what tax rates, brackets, or deductions might be at that point. Any cash distributions will not show up on the 1040 tax form. The same tax result as anything named "ROTH."

And IULs aren't only for younger folks. Many seniors can truly benefit from them as well. It's also a great CD, money market, bond, or annuity alternative.

Bill is a 70-year-old in normal health (not great) with $250,000 sitting in low-interest and taxable CDs that he wasn't planning on ever touching. We moved that money into an IUL contract all at once (single premium), with an initial death benefit of $306,000.

As you may remember, putting too much into a life policy too soon will make it a MEC contract. Rather than a TRIPLE

ZERO™ plan, it's only a "double-zero" plan. A MEC keeps 1) unlimited contributions/no income limits and 2) no stock market risk (with the lock-in and reset attributes)—but it does forfeit the tax-free nature of any distributions. However, his money will grow tax-deferred—no annual 1099 forms reported to the IRS if he doesn't take any money out of his policy.

Illustrating an annual average crediting (earnings) of just 6%—EVEN AFTER deducting ALL of the insurance policy loads, fees, and charges—the accumulation value in Bill's contract would have safely grown from $250,000 to about $373,000 in just ten years—all tax-deferred. There's little chance his CDs could do that nowadays. His cash safely grew by $123,000. His death benefit grew too, it will be $449,000 at that point.

And if Bill died in five years (age 75), his beneficiary would get about $360,000 income tax-free. In fact, his policy's cash value and death benefit will likely grow to about $705,000 and $769,000, respectively, over the first 20 years and keep increasing if he never touches the cash in the policy. Your CD money can work harder for you. You and your family deserve such.

But... if Bill ever needs or wants to get some cash out of his policy to supplement his income (say at age 85), he could do that, too. Under the same assumptions, he could take $3,300 out of his policy every month until age 100.

That's a total of $594,000 potential income for himself, plus he would still leave a death benefit of $238,000 to his loved ones. Being a MEC, however, the distributions would be taxable until his basis (the $250,000 premium).

All of those benefits came from a $250,000 single premium—moving money from a low-interest, taxable, sleepy, boring CD to a no-stock-market risk alternative. It's a great alternative to "LAZY MONEY,"—but one needs to be healthy enough to qualify for life insurance. If Bill's health didn't qualify, perhaps his wife's health would have. Or perhaps even one of his children.

Let's look at the opposite end of the age spectrum—Bill's first grandchild—a one-year-old grandson named Jacob. Unlike a ROTH, where one needs to have "earned income" to qualify to contribute to one, a 15-day-old baby in normal health can qualify for a TRIPLE ZERO™ plan. There are a few caveats, such as the parents must have life insurance on themselves and all children must be covered, etc.

I understand that babies do not need life insurance, but what better place to get them financially started and positioned for the rest of their life?

Let's see how this might play out for Jacob's future.

Bill wanted to fund Jacob's IUL at $200 a month for the next 25 years. That's a total inheritance to Jacob of $60,000 over that time. Bill will own the policy and control its cash value, naming any beneficiaries, etc., until he passes it to Jacob's ownership in the future.

For a baby of that age, this policy had an increasing death benefit that began at $100,000. But death benefit was not the primary motivation for Bill. It was to start a savings account, free of all stock market risk, that Jacob could access for any purpose, at any age—with no taxation (no pre-59½ issues that even a ROTH IRA would suffer).

Left untouched until Jacob's age 31, there might be some $195,000 of cash value in the policy with a death benefit of over $489,000. That cash could be used to fund a down payment on his first home or a business idea, or it could be simply left inside the policy. It's a perfect source of "private reserve" money that I'll write about later—allowing Jacob's savings in the IUL to do two jobs at once.

However, all that aside, should Jacob just leave the money in his TRIPLE ZERO™ plan until retirement at age 67, there should be some $2.2 million of cash value, and the death benefit should have grown to about $2.7 million to protect his own future loved ones.

There are a number of ways to improve that policy's performance, too. Jacob could continue to pay the $200 monthly premiums at age 26 himself or anytime thereafter.

What a wonderful legacy Bill is leaving for Jacob. Why aren't more insurance agents all over this type of planning? Well, the 1st year commission is only about $1,000 for this policy. For most agents, that's not worth the hours of explaining the benefits of this concept to both Bill and Jacob's parents too, plus doing all the needed paperwork.

While we're on the subject of children and IULs, let's take a moment and compare an IUL with a 529 college savings plan.

As a former practicing college funding planner, I could write pages comparing a properly structured and funded IUL to a 529 plan, but let me just mention a few reasons why many of my savvy clients will decide on using an IUL instead. Firstly, a parent or student-owned 529 plan is a "countable asset" in all financial aid formulas.

But life insurance (and annuities, too) and retirement accounts are specifically EXCLUDED assets on the FAFSA form and for all other college financial aid forms—except for about three dozen universities and colleges. A 529 plan can reduce your financial aid, whereas any permanent life insurance policy will not. That could be a big deal.

Secondly, the IUL is a self-completing plan. By that, I mean that if the "breadwinner" passes away—the death benefit will immediately complete the college savings plan. But again, the IUL can be a superior "tool" if you live.

And it does so by avoiding stock market risk along with the powerful lock and reset feature. They are valuable benefits.

Money in a 529 plan can only be accessed tax-free if it's spent on qualified educational expenses, while an IUL can be accessed for any purpose on a tax-free basis—as long as you follow the simple IRS rules.

Perhaps you'll need the cash for something before college, or your child gets a "full-ride" or even decides not to go to college at all. Yes, there are some solutions, but none of them are perfect.

An IUL has much more flexibility. And unlike a 529 plan, an IUL can avoid stock market risk while offering double-digit gains in the good years, has the annual lock-in and reset to profit from stock market rebounds—while the 529 plan is trying to make up for lost ground.

Ok, enough on 529 plans. They certainly have value, but like every other financial product, they do have their shortfalls as well.

Anyway, I could go on and on with more examples of TRIPLE ZERO™ plans and how many folks fund them, but you probably have the idea by now. There are literally 100,000+ of these types of plans bought every year to the tune of over $2 Billion dollars in brand-new policies.

And as I previously wrote, 100% of my own retirement savings are my contributions to five TRIPLE ZERO™ policies. I can't do a ROTH and, in any case, although not perfect, IULs give me almost everything I'm looking for in a place to store my money. Especially if you believe, as I do, that taxes "must" go up at some point to pay for so many huge unfunded government promises... that are still being made to us all. New COVID debt makes me even more convinced!

I'm sure by now, you have "googled" IULs, and much of what you have read about them on the internet is very different from what you are reading in this book. At the end of my book, after going through the rest of one of the Get Me to ZERO™ strategies, I'll address and dispel each of those falsehoods and myths.

Do you think I own five IULs to have made a commission from myself? No, I bought them for my lifetime benefit. Out of my own and my family's best interest. But only you can decide if an IUL would add value to your own retirement planning and help provide you and those your care most about with a truly fantastic retirement. Spending your money instead of sending it to the IRS.

Ok, to continue explaining how IULs work, I'll discuss in detail how you access your money from them. I'll then describe the Private Reserve strategy and how this feature alone can make a TRIPLE ZERO™ plan much more valuable for you and your family before retirement.

After that, I'll write about how some folks can actually use OPM (Other People's Money) to help you fund a huge TRIPLE ZERO™ plan, as well as how some business owners (and millions of other folks) can do some cool things by funding them as well—using OPM (Other People's Money). That's my Catapult strategy and there is nothing like it.

We'll add to our discussion on IULs with some worthwhile information and an additional concept to ponder.

Sequence of Returns Risk

Before I write about how to access your cash in your TRIPLE ZERO™ plan, I'd like to teach you about sequence of returns risk when you are withdrawing money from any normal account (traditional IRA/401K, or any ROTH) for income during retirement.

This is how the mutual fund company Thornburg Investment Management defines sequence of return risk: "Sequence of returns is simply the order in which returns are realized by a retiree. The consequences of a bad sequence of returns, especially early in retirement, can mean premature depletion of the portfolio. Retirees need to avoid being in the position of having to sell during inopportune market environments." In other words, taking withdrawals when the market is down. This is not an issue with IULs—as ZERO is your hero! No sequence risk.

Rob Williams, managing director of income planning at the Schwab Center for Financial Research, says, "When you're withdrawing funds at the same time that your portfolio is losing value, you can expose yourself to a phenomenon known as sequence-of-returns risk.

Annual Income = 5% of first-year value adjusted thereafter for inflation Starting Value for Portfolio A and Portfolio B = $500,000

Age	Annual Return	Annual Withdrawal	Portfolio A Year-End Value	Age	Annual Return	Annual Withdrawal	Portfolio B Year-End Value
65	N/A	$25,000	$500,000	65	N/A	$25,000	$500,000
66	-10.1%	$25,000	$424,300	66	19.4%	$25,000	$572,100
67	-13.0%	$25,000	$343,971	67	9.5%	$25,000	$601,678
68	-23.4%	$25,000	$238,585	68	-0.7%	$25,000	$572,286
69	26.4%	$25,000	$276,524	69	11.4%	$25,000	$612,469
70	9.0%	$25,000	$276,383	70	29.6%	$25,000	$768,760
71	3.0%	$25,000	$259,675	71	13.4%	$25,000	$846,851
72	13.6%	$25,000	$270,043	72	0.0%	$25,000	$821,851
73	3.5%	$25,000	$254,575	73	12.8%	$25,000	$901,884
74	-38.5%	$25,000	$131,564	74	23.5%	$25,000	$1,088,376
75	23.5%	$25,000	$137,415	75	-38.5%	$25,000	$644,460
76	12.8%	$25,000	$129,977	76	3.5%	$25,000	$642,209
77	0.0%	$25,000	$104,977	77	13.6%	$25,000	$704,678
78	13.4%	$25,000	$94,055	78	3.0%	$25,000	$700,818
79	29.6%	$25,000	$96,895	79	9.0%	$25,000	$738,822
80	11.4%	$25,000	$82,931	80	26.4%	$25,000	$908,723
81	-0.7%	$25,000	$57,326	81	-23.4%	$25,000	$671,355
82	9.5%	$25,000	$37,795	82	-13.0%	$25,000	$558,810
83	19.4%	$25,000	$20,134	83	-10.1%	$25,000	$477,147
	4.8%		$20,134		4.8%		$477,147

Huge difference

The order in which investment returns occur can have a huge impact on your assets' long-term if you are taking withdrawals from (or even adding to) your portfolio." The big risk when taking withdrawals is the negative years.

The above chart shows how the order of returns affects your eventual retirement success (not outliving your cash).

You can see that the average returns over the period are identical (4.8%). Both portfolios start at $500,000. Each person is withdrawing a constant $25,000 per year. The ONLY difference between the two portfolios is the ORDER of the returns. Portfolio A's returns are in the exact opposite order of Portfolio B.

But look at the ending values! Same average return, same withdrawal—just the <u>opposite order</u> of returns. So, keep in mind that with IULs—you never have market losses and, therefore, no sequence of returns risk!!

Accessing Your Cash

Throughout the last number of pages, I've described a number of clients, how they've funded their IULs, and the conservative projections they are looking for in terms of non-taxable supplemental cash flow during their retirement. So how do they access their cash, and why is it tax-free (assuming they follow the simple IRS rules)?

There are basically three ways to get access to your cash surrender value in your TALIC (Tax-Advantaged Life Insurance Contract)... without dying.

The first way is to take withdrawals of your basis (the amount you've paid in premiums so far). When your policy is designed to be a <u>Maximum Efficient</u> Contract (not a

MEC), you can take out your basis from the cash surrender value at any time. Since the IRS sees this as "your own money" (after-tax premiums paid), it is not taxable income.

However, in a <u>Modified Endowment</u> Contract (MEC), any earnings or interest comes out first—which would be taxable until you are down to just the basis in the contract (not taxable). As discussed, there is nothing wrong with a MEC in and of itself.

But you definitely do NOT want to have your policy become a MEC for Get Me to ZERO™ planning and tax-free income and/or lifetime access to your savings.

Nothing wrong with taking a "withdrawal" from your life insurance contract—but just understand that it is a withdrawal and not a loan. Any withdrawals from the policy can never be paid back and therefore, cannot be available for your future use (Private Reserve strategy).

The same as a ROTH, once you make a withdrawal, you can never put that money back into the ROTH. It's permanently gone from the never-taxed zone.

The second and third methods of accessing your cash in the policy are two different types of loans. They can be repaid (or not) back into the policy and would be available for you to use again and again. There are no credit checks. There are no coupon books to repay the loan. No required monthly payments at all. No amortization schedules.

As you know, when you get a loan to buy a car, a home, or purchase something on your credit card—that loan is not taxable income. The bank doesn't tell the IRS that you borrowed $50,000 to buy an SUV, nor do you pay income taxes on the bank's money because it's not income… it's a loan that needs to be repaid.

It's the same thing with taking a loan from your insurance contract. It's a loan that, if you do not repay while you're alive, it will be repaid out of the death benefit. More on this point in a moment.

One thing that gets me so mad is when an untrained insurance agent tells someone that they are borrowing their own money out of the policy and are just "paying themselves back." That is untrue. Sounds good, but they have no idea what they are talking about.

You are borrowing the money from the insurance company, and the cash surrender value in your contract is the <u>collateral</u> for the loan. Since the insurance company has full collateral (and no stock market risk of declining like a "margin" account at your broker's), there are no credit checks, no questions about what you want to use the funds for, and no loan applications. It's a pretty simple and quick process.

The insurance company is delighted to loan you money. They earn interest and are fully protected and secure with your collateral (cash value). Your loan collateral and the interest receivable are more secure than a corporate bond.

Did you know that Walt Disney took a loan out on his insurance contract to help get his company going? More recently, Doris Christopher, the founder of Pampered Chef (now owned by Warren Buffett's Berkshire Hathaway), also used a life insurance policy loan to grow her business.

Collateral is fully secured by the policy's cash value. Many more folks have started a business or weathered hard times with funds from inside their life contract.

Before I get started with this, let me say that each insurance company seems to have a different name for its loan option(s). This can be confusing, but they mostly work in one of the following two ways. Some insurers offer one loan option only; others offer 2 or 3.

The first type of policy loan is often referred to as a "wash loan." It is either a no "Net" cost loan or has a small guaranteed interest rate (usually 1% or less). The terms, and interest percentages will vary by insurer and how for many years, the policy has been in force.

Here's how a typical "wash loan" might work. On any amounts loaned from the policy, the insurance company may charge you a guaranteed interest rate of 4% while at the same time crediting the loan balance with a guaranteed 3.5% interest earned. That would leave you a net interest cost on the loan balance of just 0.5%.

The interest rates charged and credited may be different and hopefully as low as a guaranteed 0% or .25% loan cost once the policy has been owned for 6-10 years or so. In any case, it's pretty attractive.

On this loan type, it's important to note that any outstanding loans are <u>not</u> participating in any index(es) growth. So loaned amount interest credits are calculated per the above, with no chance of growth in the index(es), while un-loaned funds can have full gains (caps, spreads).

The other type of loan doesn't sound as attractive at first, but I think it is certainly so over time. Again, it goes by different names. I like the name "participating" best. I like the word "participating" because, under this loan option, your full account balances (including loans) can participate in the index growth (or a 0% return in a negative year).

How the insurance company charges interest under this method varies. Most insurers have their interest rate "floating" with an index such as the Moody's Bond Index or perhaps the Prime Rate. This can be an attractive option when interest rates have been very low) such as over the last 5-10 years. But those interest rates can go sky-high too.

There have been many periods when Moody's and similar bond indexes have had rates of 7%, 8%, 9%, and even double digits. I'm not very comfortable with being locked in forever to a loan interest rate that I have no control over. Personally, I prefer the next type of loan.

A few other policies have a guaranteed participating loan rate of 5% to 6%. All loans will always be charged that specific guaranteed interest rate—no matter the Moody's/Prime rates (lower or higher). Some have a floating loan rate that will never be lower than, say, 4%... and never higher than 6%. Depending upon interest rates in general, there is a guaranteed range of loan costs that you know in advance.

But I like this certainty of knowing how my interest will be calculated, and it has a <u>maximum</u> interest rate. I can plan for it.

So why is a loan rate of 4% or 6% potentially more attractive than a "wash loan" (maybe <1%, although I've seen wash loan net rates as high as 4% in awful policies)?

Well, I've already given you a hint. Under this loan regime, ALL of your cash value can participate in the index gains. If you believe that over time, the index will return about 7% or more on average, and your loan cost is guaranteed to be under 6%; then, you have an attractive loan arbitrage opportunity. Loan arbitrage is how your bank makes money. Pay low interest rates on CDs and lend funds out to consumers at higher rates.

If you could borrow at a guaranteed 6% and you could get an average 7% return, how much would you borrow? I'd borrow as much as I could. As long as I am pretty confident that my policy would earn more than my 6% loan costs over time. When the index gets capped out at 11% and my loan cost is 6%, I've made a 5% arbitrage profit from the loan within the policy.

I got paid a profit to take a loan. However, on the other side of the coin, if I get a 0% interest credit one year when the stock market tanked, I'd have a 6% interest rate loss that year. There's that risk/reward again.

Since December 2020, the new NAIC rules only allow IUL illustrations to "show" or project a maximum of .5% loan arbitrage on loan balances. But I believe the reality will be about 1.5%+ over time—so the tax-free cash flow should be higher than projected when I do illustrations for new clients. But again, I always like to make conservative projections and plan to beat them.

The 15, 20, or 25-year crediting history of many of the indexes used in the IULs have historical average rates of returns that exceed +7.5%. Some are well over 8.25%. So, I feel pretty comfortable projecting future income distributions using +7% average interest earnings over time

—especially with a guaranteed maximum loan interest rate.

Very few insurers will let you switch from one type of loan (wash loan) to the "participating" loan as often as once a year. That gives you the best of both worlds. You can use the wash loan when you think the markets will go down (protection in the few bad years) and use the participating loan when markets are doing well (most years) to take advantage of the potential positive loan arbitrage.

As I'm writing this page, I just saw a commercial on CNBC talking about margin loan rates on brokerage accounts like Schwab, Fidelity, etc. If you're not familiar with brokerage account margin loans, you can generally borrow up to 50% of your stock holdings at fluctuating rates. Those rates just mentioned in the commercial were over 7.5%, and those interest rates are not locked in. They can go higher or lower at the brokerage firm's discretion.

But unlike a margin account at your broker, you will never get a margin call from your insurance company because of a market crash (or one of your stocks crashed like Enron) since market losses do not occur in the IUL like they can (and will) happen in the stock market.

You will get a brokerage margin call when the value of your loan balance is more than 50% of the value of your portfolio. So, if you borrowed $75,000 from your $150,000 brokerage account and the portfolio value drops to $140,000, you'll need to add another $10,000 right away or they'll start selling your positions from under you. There were lots of margin calls in early February 2018 when the market dipped about 10% within a few days from all-time highs. And the same thing again during the COVID crash.

I had a margin loan called back in 2002. They told me to deposit another $20,000 by the next day. I did, and then I had to send another $6,000 the day after that. That was enough. I closed the account!

Anyway, of course, any loan or withdrawal from a life policy will lower the net death benefit to your loved ones. That makes common sense. If you repay the loan, the death benefit gets restored as well.

And here's the most important thing to know and keep forever in your mind about IUL loans. You <u>never</u> want your policy to lapse for any reason, including taking too much money out of it. <u>You MUST die with your policy in force</u>, and a death benefit must be paid to your beneficiaries. They will get whatever is left over after paying back the loan (retirement cash flow) and any accrued interest due.

If your policy lapses before you do (death), all loans and interest will become taxable. The insurance company will send you a 1099, and believe me when I say that you will not want to pay that tax bill. To prevent that from ever happening, most policies have an "over-loan" protection rider, which would pay off the loan and interest and reduces the death benefit down to $10,000 or something so that you die with that death benefit in force and never, ever get a taxable 1099 form.

Of the two loan types, the "wash loan" is the most conservative and will likely produce the lowest lifetime tax-free cash flow, while the participating type-loan will offer the most potential for higher income. They both have their place, and that's why I love the few IULs that allow you to switch loan methods as often as every policy year.

Again, many IULs do not allow you to switch loan types at all, while others may only allow one loan switch during your lifetime. That's not optimal. All things being equal – loan flexibility is a huge advantage. Not only while taking lifetime tax-free monthly distributions during your retirement but in conjunction with the next chapter as well. OK, we're finally at the Private Reserve Strategy!

Private Reserve Strategy

Now that you have a good understanding of how policy loans work in IULs. I'd like to explain the Private Reserve strategy that I've referenced many times. In a nutshell, this strategy revolves around having your savings work for you in two places at once—by using a 2nd type of arbitrage. It's the same way that banks money. Pay depositors a tiny interest and loan out their money at much higher rates.

When I wrote about the potential loan arbitrage above (earning 7% in the policy with a loan maximum of 6%), that was primarily about how you can increase your retirement cash flow (100% TAX-FREE) from policy loans from a TRIPLE ZERO™ plan. Since your accumulation value (the value invested in the various indexing options) is never going down because of loan distributions (although your loan balance increases each year), you can profit from the 1% positive loan arbitrage in this example.

But the private reserve strategy is used while we are accumulating the savings in your policy—not during the Get Me to ZERO™ tax-free income phase of the plan. It is meant to add to your total wealth along the way—in a manner that is not possible with a ROTH 401K or ROTH IRA (or any retirement plan for that matter). It's a strategy that allows you to have your policy funds earning returns in two places at once. It's another kind of financial leverage.

First and foremost, you need to understand that this strategy is only for serious savers and investors—not spenders. You want your money to grow in two places and not just grow in one (IUL) and be spent along the way... leaving you with a loan balance in your policy that will decrease (or perhaps even eliminate) your supplemental tax-free cash flow in retirement. It's about investing wisely... versus spending.

So, as just mentioned, when you take a participating loan out of your IUL, it does not reduce your accumulation value earning interest (but a wash loan does). So, there is more upside with that type of loan, while there are times (when you anticipate a bear market that the wash loan is a great one to switch to if your IUL allows it).

You'll also recall that the loan comes from the insurance company's checkbook—with your cash surrender value being used as the collateral. That's why there are no loan applications, credit checks, explanations of why you want the money, etc. For simplicity's sake here, let's assume that you own an IUL with a fixed (or at least a capped loan interest rate) of 6% (the highest guaranteed loan rate).

Collateral capacity is the amount of funds you have available in your life insurance plan to borrow against. The more you fund and the longer you own your IUL, the more collateral capacity you'll have. It's a valuable resource for you and your family. Treat it wisely.

The ability to access your capital, no matter what the economy is doing, whether you are employed or not, without completing invasive and personal credit applications or credit checks, and without questions about what you want to use the money for is a beautiful feeling. And this ability to get capital within a week or two can make you wealthier.

In the private reserve strategy, you can borrow most of your cash surrender value in the policy and <u>invest</u> it somewhere else that you believe will easily earn more then the 6% interest cost (NET after paying taxes) since this loaned money is now outside of the "tax-free" zone.

The indexing strategies in the IUL with the 0% floor (no losses from the markets) along with the powerful combination of locking in and protecting all prior gains from market losses (lock-in) and the "reset" mechanism... will give you something close to or better than an average of 7% gross interest crediting per year over time.

The indexes in the policy are going to earn what they are going to earn. Probably more than 7%, but maybe less over a bad 10-year period. Borrowing money from inside the policy to invest in a second place won't affect your IUL one bit—as long as you pay the insurer and interest back.

The financial "hurdle" that you need to clear in the private reserve strategy is how much, after paying income/capital gain taxes, will your second investment make you. In this example, the after-tax net earnings hurdle must be over 6% a year (or whatever the interest rate you owe the insurance company) policy loan cost.

Remember that you'll want to pay the insurance company back with interest (put the loan amounts back into your IUL). And since you want to pay the insurance company back, your second investment should be very reliable. I would never invest in penny stocks, raw land, Bitcoin (or any digital currency), etc. with proceeds from a policy loan. Pigs get fat, and hogs get slaughtered.

If you want to speculate on any of those or a long list of other high-risk investments, I would never recommend using ANY loan to do it. In my opinion, that's simply reckless. This is your retirement money!

Could you pay off high-interest credit card debt with a 6% loan from your IUL? Sure, that may make sense if your credit card interest rate is 15% or more. That's a 9% positive arbitrage. However, what my experience as a financial planner has taught me is that once many folks pay off their credit card loans with a HELOC, 401K, or any other lower-cost loan, these folks tend to run the credit cards right back up again and are now in a worse position. They owe money to the HELOC, credit union, or insurer… and have brand new credit card debt to boot!

That's not a good thing. It's a good idea gone wrong! Would I use my policy to finance a car like so many agents are pushing now? Absolutely not. My current car loan is at 2.15%. I wouldn't use the collateral capacity inside my policies for something like that. It's much too valuable – even if I couldn't get a car loan for under 8%. Personally, I won't take out a loan from any of my policies unless I'm pretty confident that I'll get an <u>after-tax return</u> of at least

10%-12% in 12 months or less. I don't want to speculate and take undue risks. Again, pigs get fat, and hogs get slaughtered. No need to be greedy or reckless.

The following is NOT investment advice nor a recommendation. But I know many people (my clients, my advisor friend's clients, etc.) that have used their collateral capacity to invest in real estate rehabs, real estate flipping, hard money loans, and tax liens (all with the underlying property as collateral—an added layer of protection).

I've heard of using loans for invoice factoring, a car dealer who finances cars. One retired car salesman buys cars at auctions (using policy loans) and sells them. I'm told that he has "flipped" as many as six cars in a month using one policy loan. He's still earning returns inside his policy.

With the stock markets up so high now, I would never borrow from my policy to invest in stocks at these levels. But my thinking might change after the next crash. One of my close advisor friends bought McDonald's stock in 2009 with a policy loan and reaped some very good profits over the next 18-24 months. He thought the risk was worth the reward. I would have diversified into more than one stock.

But he will <u>not</u> recommend to his own clients that they ever invest in the stock market with proceeds from a policy loan. <u>Neither will I</u>. The point here is to be as wise as you can with your collateral capacity. Invest/flip/rehab in something you know about—especially if it has collateral (real estate, car, boats, etc.) with a short turnaround (no longer than 12-24 months). The faster, the better.

At the least, make sure that you'll get your loan amount back if your deal wasn't profitable, so you'd only lose the interest paid to the insurance company. Cut your losses and move on to the next opportunity. Profit from your opportunities and learn from your mistakes.

Meanwhile, you are enjoying uninterrupted compounding and growth in your TRIPLE ZERO™ policy.

Your loaned money never left the policy, and it continues to grow based on the performance of the index strategies you chose. The cash value is simply the loan collateral.

Before I go on, I'll just make a quick comparison with a ROTH. I love ROTHs, as you know, but like an IUL, they are not perfect and have shortcomings like everything else in this world. No IRA (ROTH or traditional) can be used for loan collateral. It's against the law. So, there is no way to do the private reserve strategy with a ROTH or any IRA.

Once you take money out of a ROTH, you can never put it back. It's gone from the tax-free zone forever. ROTH funds have no way of increasing your wealth in two places at once. Your savings are either growing inside of your ROTH… or if you take it out (it's now taxable)—not both places.

One of my original IUL mentor's clients had over 1 million dollars of cash value sitting in his IUL—which, as you'll see in a moment, is the absolute best "parking garage" for your money. At the height of the last financial crisis, he had a great opportunity to buy a foreclosure on Hilton Head beach. The condo was worth over $625,000 back in 2007.

If he could get the money within ten business days, he could buy it for $478,000. He simply faxed the insurance company, who quickly sent him the money (since it is fully collateralized with his cash value) so he could close on the condo and take advantage of this great deal.

It had a long history of earning nearly $43,000 in net annual rental income—that's a 9% cash-on-cash annual return on the rent. That more than covers his 6% interest cost to the insurer. And that doesn't include any potential appreciation when the recession ended.

So he can simultaneously earn rental income from the condo (pay back the loan to the policy over time) while continuing to get potential double-digit gains from his IUL policy as the stock market rebounds from the last recession (past gains were locked in and the indexes reset).

He can then sell the condo in a few years at a big profit when the real estate market gets better or keep it by refinancing it with a traditional mortgage and paying back the full policy loan within a few years. Put the funds back into your financial "parking garage" and wait for the next profitable business opportunity to come along.

Like all policy loans, there are no structured loan repayments. No coupon books. No loan amortization schedules. He doesn't need to pay the policy loan back at all... or even any interest either. But not doing so would likely put his plans for invisible retirement cash flow from his policy in jeopardy. Always pay back your private reserve loans—with interest!

No other "lender" will give you more flexible repayment terms than your personal TRIPLE ZERO™ can. Paying back that loan principal and interest replaces your collateral capacity, giving you access to capital to take advantage of opportunity after opportunity. All the while, your funds inside of the TRIPLE ZERO™ plan earn 0%-12%+ or so each year.

Using your IUL as a "parking garage for your cash" and as a private reserve account can really TURBO-charge your net worth. It's a safe parking place that you don't have to wait until you retire to use. You can get profitable pre-retirement access, benefits, and flexibility that you cannot get anywhere else (at least not on the same terms).

Here's another crucial financial point to learn, embrace, and teach your children about making major purchases. Many wealthy folks tell me they pay cash for everything (except perhaps their real estate). I guess there's nothing wrong with being debt-free. I certainly oppose taking on consumer debt to fund one's lifestyle.

But they are forgetting an essential financial truth about paying cash for everything. Are you ready to learn it?

You <u>finance</u> EVERY SINGLE BIG THING you buy! Because you either PAY interest to finance or lease those things... or you LOSE the interest and investment income that you could have earned if you'd kept your own money invested instead. You either <u>pay</u> interest or <u>earn</u> interest.

Now, most folks think that they SAVE interest by paying cash for purchases, and that is true. But that's only half of the story. The whole truth is that "you either pay someone else interest to use their money, or you lose the interest you would have earned by using your own cash instead." This is an economic law—a financial truth.

Unless the funds you use to pay for something were hidden under your mattress and not earning any interest, you are actually giving up all the interest/growth those savings would have made by using your own money and not financing. Not only do you lose interest this year, but your lost interest is compounded year after year after year.

That's called lost "opportunity cost." Of course, your savings have to be earning higher interest than your interest cost to consider financing as described. But just know that you're always financing— (paying/losing interest) one way or the other on any major purchase.

With the private reserve strategy, your funds inside of the policy (assuming you are using a "participating loan") continue uninterrupted compounding—without having to give up an opportunity to take advantage of other select and carefully thought-out investment opportunities.

Assuming just a 2%-2.5% private reserve arbitrage (your money invested in two places at once), you could add up to $100,000 or much more wealth over 20-30 years.

Let's change gears again and get back to the TRIPLE ZERO™ plans.

But I heard that "life insurance is a bad investment!" Well, life insurance is <u>not</u> an investment. It's life insurance with a death benefit and premium payments.

However, based on what you've read so far, would you agree that it is a pretty good place to store and build your wealth that also offers very favorable tax advantages? And with the IUL structure, is it a place to avoid stock market risk while having the potential for double-digit gains when the market does well?

From what you've read so far, if it wasn't called "life

insurance" and there was no death benefit (that you do pay for), would this type of "parking place" for your money be pretty compelling as a long-term supplement to all your ROTH strategies?

The death benefit is what gives life insurance all of its many tax advantages. Tax advantages have been part of cash value life policies since 1913 when income taxes began in the U.S. And I've never known a life insurance agent to have been kicked out of a house when delivering a significant death benefit check to a beneficiary. Not once.

How much life insurance would you want if it was free? All you could get! I would, too. So, it's not life insurance that folks aren't excited about; it's paying for it— (usually for the benefit of somebody else at our death).

With the TRIPLE ZERO™ strategy, we reduce those mortality costs to the lowest possible (assuming your policy is structured to be as efficient as possible) for your own "living benefits."

That's right, in addition to the death benefit component (especially in the early years), we try to maximize the benefits to you and your family while you're alive and well. That brings us to the next potential benefit of an IUL (and other life insurance policies).

Long-Term Care Benefits (LTC)

It seems that everybody who knows how much long-term care costs (in a home, assisted living, or nursing home) is concerned about if they and/or a family member will need care for an extended period of time someday. How will they handle that potential financial burden? It's probably the most feared but least prepared-for "risk" that too many Americans have. And that fear is well-placed and valid.

When I was 40, I bought my own traditional LTC policy. The smartest thing I ever did (assuming I don't die in my sleep). But today, these policies are much more expensive and harder to qualify for based on your health.

And there is no getting around the "use it… or lose it" nature of traditional LTC insurance policies. Traditional LTC insurance sales today is a fraction of what they were in the late 1990s.

But that doesn't make the risk of you or your spouse needing LTC someday go away. The risk of needing care and its potential costs is still there.

There are many life insurance policies that offer an alternative to traditional LTC insurance policies. And some annuities do, too. They require much bigger premiums, but at least there is a benefit to the family if you die never needing LTC care—the death benefit or annuity account value. I won't go into all the types of life insurance policies that also offer some sort of LTC benefit—over and above the actual death benefit in this book.

But what I will do, as appropriate here, is briefly discuss general information as to the LTC benefit in some IUL policies. Some have no-cost LTC benefits... while others charge a cost for an LTC "rider."

There are basically two types of LTC benefits in many TRIPLE ZERO™ policies should you need assistance in 2 of the 6 Activities of Daily Living (eating, bathing, toileting, dressing, transferring, and incontinence) for a period that is expected to last at least 90 days... or have some type of cognitive impairment such as Alzheimer's.

In one type of LTC benefit, the IUL insurer would advance you a "discounted" death benefit in the amount of perhaps 2%, 3%, or 4% a month to help pay for your care at home or in a facility. Why discounted?

Well, since the IUL is a life insurance policy, it was priced on your likely death somewhere in your 80s. If you have a stroke at 68 and need care, they will be paying out part of your death benefit about 15 years too early. So, the IULs with no-cost LTC benefits will typically discount the death benefit (based on a formula) and pay that 2%-4% monthly advance of the reduced death benefit since they are paying it way earlier than your original life expectancy.

The IUL policies that offer an LTC rider for a charge (which reduces your policy cash accumulation) will <u>not</u> discount the death benefit when they advance you the funds to help pay for your care at home or in a licensed facility. In either case, every advance of your death benefit will reduce both your cash value/eventual death benefit.

If you are primarily interested in having LTC protection on your IUL policy (rather than income), I would consider paying for the rider (which is a cost drag on the accumulation value). However, here's why I wouldn't pay for an LTC rider on a TRIPLE ZERO™-designed plan.

By definition, the TRIPLE ZERO™ plan is designed to minimize the death benefit—particularly by the time you are taking tax-free cash flow out of the policy. So, there won't be much difference in the amount of your death benefit and the cash surrender value in your policy.

You'll likely be better off just keeping the tax-free distributions coming in. Initially, it was structured to supplement ROTH income and reduce your income tax burden to as close to ZERO as possible.

In the TRIPLE ZERO™, <u>unless</u> you have an LTC care "event" in the early years of the policy, neither a paid LTC feature nor one included at no charge is going to be that big of a benefit. But just like if you die early in the early years, having an LTC need with an LTC benefit in the early years can be of great value! But under normal circumstances, the LTC rider is not nearly as valuable as many insurance agents make it out to be.

Those agents try to "sell" someone on the idea of having both LTC protection (when they are old and more likely to need it) and the tax-free cash flow at the same time, either don't understand how the LTC benefit actually works or... well, I'll just leave it at that. No further comment.

Trade-in the Old for the New?

For some strange reason, life insurance is the only industry that tries to keep people from "trading in" their obsolete products for a newer, improved version. Maybe it's time for a policy upgrade.

You may have a whole life or some type of universal life insurance policy in force already. Even though you are older now, it sometimes makes absolute financial sense to do a tax-free exchange (1035X) from the old kinds of policies to a new one with new benefits and lower mortality costs because we are living longer than before.

If you already own a cash-value life insurance policy, it may (or may not) be to your advantage to consider doing a 1035 tax-free exchange of an old policy into a TRIPLE ZERO™ plan if it's your desire to pay less future taxes or even to just help financially protect against an LTC event.

Basically, once you get health approved by the new insurer, you can instruct them to request the funds in your old policy be transferred directly to the new one (which would cancel the old policy).

The CSO mortality tables are put together by the American Academy of Actuaries, which is an 18,500+ member professional association whose mission is to serve the public and the U.S. actuarial profession.

The internal insurance costs in all life insurance policies are largely determined by the CSO mortality table used. But over the years, as our nation's longevity has increased, these mortality tables have changed—getting a lot less expensive (by 30% to 50% or more).

From 2009-2019, all life policies issued must have used the 2001 CSO mortality tables. Any policy issued before 2001 (and through 2008) is burdened with older, outdated life expectancy mortality costs (1980 CSO mortality rates). If your policy was issued before 1980, those CSO mortality costs (set back in 1958) are another 30% more expensive. The new 2017 CSO tables are in effect as of Jan. 1st, 2020.

A new IUL can have less expensive internal mortality costs (using the more recent CSO life expectancy tables) even though you are older now. The bottom line is that your current life policy (even an outdated IUL) is likely costing you too much.

But more importantly, it may be leaving other "new and improved living benefits" off the table for you and your family. That's true even if your annual premiums are "paid-up" or are being paid out of the policy cash values or from dividends.

Moving your old policy to a new TRIPLE ZERO™ one could improve your retirement cash flow. Or you can get a larger death benefit, stop ongoing premium payments… or get a new policy with enhanced Long-Term Care benefits at no out-of-pocket cost to you.

Plus, unlike an older Universal Life or Whole Life policy, you get the chance to safely earn up to 8%-12%+ when the markets do well and benefit from the lock-in and reset.

Why settle for a low fixed-rate return when you can have the chance to earn up to double-digits when the markets do well? Or take advantage of much better policy loan terms. For example, I just saw an IUL (issued in 2008) with a 4% guaranteed "wash loan" cost, but it's at "only 2%" now. Yikes! Are you kidding me—a 4% guaranteed "wash loan?" We started a 1035 exchange that day.

You just might need to have your old policy carefully analyzed to see what may be best for you today. Based on my experience, you'll likely be very pleased with the policy analysis and your options to make a substantial policy improvement—if you are healthy enough.

Be confident that all of your existing life policies are pulling their weight and that your family would not be better served with a brand new one with better interest earnings strategies, loan terms, etc.

FYI: If you would like, my team does in-depth life insurance policy "audits" every month at no cost and without any obligation. Just let me know if you are interested. No medical exam is needed to do our initial due diligence report. Of course, never, ever cancel your current policy until the new one is fully in force.

I know you have been waiting to learn about Catapult plans to pour gasoline on your retirement savings planning. Well, here we go...

Catapult Your TRIPLE ZERO™

The following pages will probably be of most interest to very successful people (household income of $150,000+) who will find this unique program a game-changer.

Financing life insurance premiums has been around for decades. Financing has been (and continues to be) mostly for the wealthy—those with a net worth of at least $5 million (excluding their primary residence) up to $10+ BILLION. It's OPM (Other People's Money) in action. They say, "Why use your own cash when you don't have to?"

I have these other financing programs available, too. But they all involve heavy financial underwriting, personal loan guarantees, and the posting of significant outside collateral (or a line of credit). But they do allow for more leverage. And that's what we're really talking about—leveraging your significant resources.

Why use your own funds (which hopefully the policy is earning much more than the cost of borrowing) to pay for life insurance? It's called Premium Financing or Premium Funding—and it is big business for some life insurers. Most "big dollar" premium finance programs (there are a few great ones and several ones I would not recommend to my worst enemy—so buyer beware!)—are used for estate planning, buy/sell agreements, or advanced other financial planning. Our team does these, too.

But through a unique program, which I'll refer to here as "Catapult" (**not its real name, so no need to google it**), which uses OPM to help fund a tax-free cash flow during retirement (and other needs too) to those with a net worth of just $1,000,000 (exclusive of your home) or $400,000+ of annual household income (or some combination).

One Catapult IUL insurer accepts a much lower net worth of $250,000 assets (excluding your home) and income of $150,000+), but I don't like that policy quite as much.

If you think about it, wealthy people have always used

"leverage" to increase their assets, whether borrowing to purchase or expand a business, buy real estate, etc. They use their good credit and borrowing capacity.

Just last week, I was at a conference speaking with a CPA/attorney friend who has been involved with premium financing for his clients for about 15 years. He is now working with a billionaire Wall Street guy and his wife, who are looking to finance $400 million of death benefits ($200 million on each spouse) for estate planning purposes. Who would want to write those colossal premium checks from their checking account? Nobody—hence the attractiveness of premium financing.

The bank(s) will loan the money to them to pay up to 100% of the needed premiums, but they will need to post additional collateral (beyond the cash value in the policies) and pay interest to get the deal done. They will not only be underwritten for their health but also financially (and they'll need to provide annual financial statements to the lenders for as long as the loans are in place). Their other collateral is still under their control—earning themselves a return (though the lenders require it "just in case").

Anyway, let's take a quick look at how a Catapult program would look for someone "like most of us" and its advantages over traditional premium finance. In many ways, it's actually better than what the multi-millionaires get. For one, the policy is the <u>only</u> collateral needed!

First of all, to qualify for Catapult, you need to be age 60 or under, and be in normal health (and perhaps without any tobacco/nicotine use for the last 3-5 years).

Just like any TRIPLE ZERO™ plan, the minimum death benefit for the maximum-funded contract is based on your age, sex, and health. We're simply getting approximately 3:1 matching premiums from bank loans.

You pay about 50% of the premium for only five years. A lender will loan the other 50% or so for the same five years. For years 6-10, the bank will loan 100% of the premium, and then the policy funding is complete. We then let the cash value grow with the indexing strategies.

TURBO-CHARGE You Savings! CATAPULT Uses 3:1 OPM
How Does Leveraging Help?
More Cash To Buy More Current and Future Benefits!

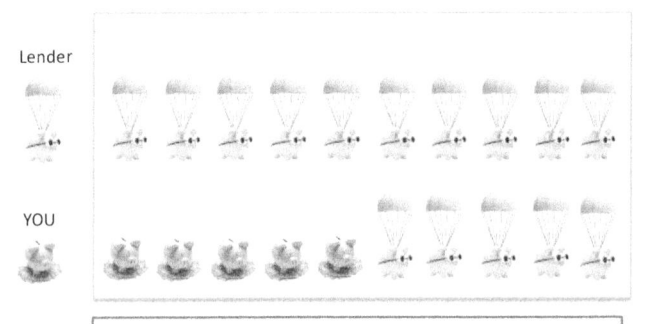

Lender

YOU

The CATAPULT Plan requires YOU to pay only 5 annual payments

What are the minimum premiums out-of-your-pocket (50% or so) to maximum fund the Catapult policy? For example, the minimum premium to maximum-fund a $625,000 initial and increasing death benefit for a 60-year-old male in great health would be about $40,000 a year for those five years. For a 50-year-old female in average health, the minimum premium is about $25,000 a year (for 5 years only) with a lower death benefit. A 35-year-old male in top health—the lowest is about $22,000/year.

Benefits of Leverage (OPM)

The Power of Leverage	Self-funded Policy	CATAPULT
Your Contribution Per Year (Years 1-5)	$48,950	$47,600
Your Trust Fees Per Year (Years 1-5)	$0	$1,350
Your Total Annual Contributions (Years 1-5)	$48,950	$48,950
Annual Potential Policy Distributions during Retirement (age 65-90)	$48,000	$92,000 *
Total Potential Policy Distributions	$1,248,000	$2,392,000
Initial Death Benefit	$725,000	$1,500,000
Policy Potential Death Benefit/Living Benefits (at age 90)	$392,948	$1,253,755 *

45-year-old male in great health
Annual cost for ONLY 5 years = $48,950 (Total Cost of $244,750)
$1.5 million initial death benefit
* Projected Annual Distributions of $92,000/year (Nearly $2.4 million TAX-FREE Distributions)
With a Residual Death Benefit of $1.2 million at the age of 90

Above is an example of a 45-year-old male contractor in great health putting in less than $49,000 a year (for only 5 years) for a $1.5M initial death benefit. The bank loans the other half of the premium for those five years.

Then, the bank loans the full premium for years 6-10. Now, it's paid up. No more premiums. Then we just let the policy cash value grow.

The bank loan is paid off in about year 15 from funds within the policy (cash value). The client is now 60 and can take a lower income than shown then... OR wait to age 65 and start taking those TAX-FREE distributions.

Of course, if he waits a few more years, he should be able to take out an even higher income than projected.

Catapult is unique in that there are no loan applications or credit checks—you don't even sign a loan document. However, you still must meet the minimum net worth requirements of the life insurer. They want to be sure it's an appropriate program for you and that you can easily pay your 50% share of the premiums for the first five years.

Why would a bank do that? Because they have 100% collateral in the cash value of the policy. They are fully protected and can offer a loan rate of something like SOFR plus 1.75%. They have virtually zero financial risk and are willing to make these loans all day long.

Since about 2004, the company that sponsors the Catapult program (and others) currently has $4 Billion of premium financing loans on the books (they administer the programs while about 15 top-tier banks are the lenders).

The banks make the program sponsors "stress-test" the policy to the extreme while the loan is outstanding. They test it against the great depression period for bear markets, where 9 of the first 14 years would have earned a zero percent return (the floor).

On the other end of the stress test, they use the high 1980s interest rate period and see what that would do to the loan and accrued interest vs. the loan collateral. In both scenarios, the banks are satisfied that their loan is secure, and the collateral of cash value is enough to offer excellent loan terms.

Anyway, after the ten years of policy funding is complete, the cash is then allowed to grow for another 5 years or so.

Although you can decide to walk away from the policy at any time until the loan and accrued interest are paid off, you cannot use this policy for the Private Reserve strategy since the bank has a first lien on your cash value and death benefit. For some folks, that can be a downside to Catapult—no access to your IUL cash (no Private Reserve) until the loan is paid off (anytime) or you decide to exit the plan. But you're already using leverage—OPM.

If you happen to die during this period, the bank loan and accrued interest will be paid off, and your beneficiaries get the full remaining death benefit. But Catapult is designed for you to live a very long time and enjoy a tax-free income.

In about year 15, the cash value inside the policy pays off the bank loans. Catapult plans are built to add from 45% to 65% more tax-free retirement cash flow than the same policy not using any OPM. That could add $100,000s or more distributions over a long life. On top of all that additional tax-free cash flow, the death benefit is much greater from day one and over the life of the policy.

Historically, the bank loan costs are 1% to 1.5% less then the interest credited to the policy (net of expenses) over those 15 years. The benefit of bank loans to leverage your own premium contributions will add an impressive boost to your future invisible retirement cash flow.

Where do folks get the money to fund their share of the Catapult premiums for the first five years? From several sources (just like any regular TRIPLE ZERO™ plan): discretionary after-tax income, diverting "above the match" contributions from a 401K, use funds in a taxable brokerage account, an inheritance, after-tax cash from a 72(t), etc.

Here's an out-of-the-box thought to dramatically improve the Catapult results. Many business owners expect to sell their business 10-25 years in the future. Or real estate owners who want to cash out of their properties at some point. Or someone is expecting a sizable inheritance. Where do these folks put the proceeds from any of those events to stay out of taxable accounts and get into the never-taxed zone?

You can't put them in a ROTH—or traditional IRA since they only allow small contributions. You could use those funds to pay the taxes on a ROTH conversion, but you'd likely have a bunch of money left over. How else could you get this money into your Get Me to ZERO™ plan?

Well, if it were me, I'd seriously consider paying off the Catapult bank loans... rather than using cash value from inside the policy. That would allow the proceeds from any of the above events to go right into the tax-free zone. Each circumstance would be different, but it wouldn't surprise me that doing this would double the lifetime tax-free distributions from the Catapult policy. It would certainly be worth taking a closer look at.

One final point about Catapult. Catapult has a sister program (let's call it C-Catapult) that looks just like what you've read above. It's for C-Corp businesses and non-profits entities who want to recruit, reward, and retain top talent (executives, college coaches, etc.). Or it can even apply to 1099 independent contractors for endorsement deals (think Tiger Woods and Nike). Here's the difference— instead of the employ**ee** funding 50% of the premiums for the first five years, out of their own pocket, their "employ**er**" <u>lends</u> them that money instead.

You already know that a loan is not taxable to the employee or 1099 contractor, so they are getting untaxed dollars to go into their TRIPLE ZERO™ plan, which, after the bank loans are paid off, will be completely in the zero-tax zone. The employ**ee** put none of their own money in this part of their Get Me to ZERO™ strategy—with a huge death benefit to protect their loved ones too. Pretty cool.

And the employ**er** who wanted to give them a "signing bonus" to bring them on the team, or a performance bonus, etc.—what do they get out of the deal? It's very attractive for them as well as you'll see.

When an employ**er** pays a bonus to an employee, it's an expense. That money is gone forever. But when they make a loan, it becomes an asset (an account receivable) on their balance sheet—that actually earns a little interest (income). Think of it as a 30-40-year bond.

And since that bonus is no longer an expense to the corporation, what just happened to profits? They went up! What happened to the asset side of their balance sheet? There was no financial effect at all. The account receivable just replaces the cash spent on funding the premium.

When does the company get its loan repaid? It's repaid out of part of the death benefit when the employee passes away. Maybe some 30-40 years down the road—but they've been accruing interest along the way. The employee's family gets the rest of the death benefit in addition to all of the tax-free retirement cash flow they'd get in any TRIPLE ZERO™ or Catapult policy.

Ok, we've spent about 105 pages explaining why I believe you should strive to pay ZERO income taxes (or as close as possible) in retirement. There are only three powerful strategies to help get you there: ROTH contributions, ROTH conversions and maximum-funded life insurance.

Do you fully understand the nuts and bolts of the TRIPLE ZERO™ plan? You have ZERO income/contribution limits, which allow you to fund the retirement lifestyle that you are looking forward to while protecting your family along the way. So, what you want to have to happen... will actually happen—whether you're around or not!

ZERO taxes (protects you from tax increases) and ZERO market risk (which means NO SEQUENCE of returns risk).

Again, rising taxes should concern all high-earner. We all have to pay our fair share. But they're coming after US!

Did you know that 91% of Americans earn less than $100,000 per year? That may surprise many of you. But here's what I really want you to think about for a moment. If most people don't have a lot of income to tax (and only 9% have income exceeding $100,000); who will the government be most likely to tax more?

I believe it's the folks with the highest income that are going to be taxed more and more. Just my opinion, but millionaires have income. The poor don't. That's where the

REAL money is for the government to tax. You also might see "goodbye to low capital gains rates" too. And maybe, goodbye step-up-in-basis as well. Just a thought.

3 Half-Truths and Misconceptions

As promised earlier in the book, I'd like to address what you'll likely find when you google IULs. Of course, you can believe what you'd like.

I'm just here to tell you that if I believed any of that misinformation on the internet, I would not own five IULs—with those being 100% of my own retirement plan. Not what I'd recommend to most folks, but that's what's best for me and my goals in my personal situation.

Before I get started, let me pronounce that an IUL is not a guaranteed product. Of course, there are some guaranteed elements in the policy. But just like there are not any return guarantees in your 401K or ROTH, there are no guarantees related to interest crediting in your IUL.

As previously stated, you are guaranteed to never lose money because of market declines, and there is real value in that. If you are seeking a guaranteed product, don't purchase an IUL—buy a whole life policy.

But keep in mind that the dividend in a whole life policy is never guaranteed. And without those non-guaranteed dividends, that policy doesn't look good at all! I'd say they look horrible without those "projected" dividends.

If you happen to work with any life agent that says something like, "All you have to do is put in "X dollars for Y years, and then you are guaranteed to be able to pull out Z dollars of tax-free cash flow," then run like hell away from him/her. It may be likely, but it's not guaranteed.

They should be saying something like, "I know one thing for sure. This illustration is wrong. The future is not going to look exactly like this since we know that you are not going to get exactly 6% returns every single year for the next 40-60 years. That's just not going to happen.

This illustration shows you putting in "X dollars for Y years and then taking out Z dollars of tax-free cash flow using a 7% AVG. return every year—no zeros, no double-digit returns." You might average 7% over your policy's life.

Based on the past 20-year history of IULs, you'll likely average about 7% returns over time—perhaps as much as 7.5% or 9%+. And some years with big double-digit returns. When the market tanks, you get the 0% floor that year. (Thank goodness for that protection and the index reset!)

And there will be years when we'll hit the cap on some index strategies. And some years, we'll get nearly all the index's gain (over the spread) and earn 20% or more.

But we'll never, ever get exactly 7% each and every year.

1) Insurance Costs and Policy Expenses are high.

Yes, there are costs taken out of your premiums to pay for the death benefit and all other costs associated with the life insurance policy. There is no getting around that. So, this is a half-truth. But let's examine the other half. But these expenses are much cheaper than paying taxes!

First of all, your agent should show you exactly where each dollar of your policy expenses is going. They can do that when they run an illustration. Most do not. What you'll see are these costs are very high during the early years (making the first 10-15 years of the policy illustration look awful).

In the early years, your IRRs are not attractive at all due to the bulk of the policy expenses being front-loaded. But as I alluded to earlier in the book, a maximum funded TRIPLE ZERO™ plan that is designed right under the MEC line could have cumulative tax-free IRRs of 6.5%, 7%, or higher over 25 or 35+ years. That's because the expenses drop to a dribble the longer the policy is in force.

So, the good half of this half-truth is that over time, an IUL will likely have lower cumulative annual costs (less than 0.9%) than a professionally managed brokerage account or ROTH.

And you do get something for those costs—a tax-free death benefit! Meaningful protection for the ones you love, and who depend upon you. Don't discount this benefit.

2) Policy costs are not guaranteed. It's possible they could rise. This is true, but there is more to the story.

While that cannot happen with whole life contracts because the costs are at the absolute highest level from its inception. And if the board of the whole life insurer wants to reduce those costs in any year (most years) for policyholders, they can declare a "dividend."

That's not a dividend like a stock would give to shareholders (which is taxable), but legally a return of excess premium. It's not taxed since you're only getting your own money back. But if this is a concern, then let's look at a whole life policy.

The "Guaranteed Page" of the IUL illustration shows you the worst-case scenario. This worst-case scenario could only happen if BOTH: 1) you get zero % returns for each of the next 30 years and 2) the day you get your new policy, the insurer informs you they have raised the policy and/or mortality costs to the highest allowed by the contract.

But the guaranteed page also assumes that you do nothing about it. You just stick your head in the sand and watch your policy fall to pieces.

Would you do nothing at all if you got a letter about rising policy costs... or the market was going down and crediting zero % returns year after year after year?

Come on. Nobody is that stupid. First of all, none of the carriers that I use have ever raised policy expenses for existing contracts. But they do have that right.

Second of all, most agents do not even know that there is something that can be done to fix this. But the guaranteed page of the illustration assumes you and your agent do nothing at all for 10-30 years. Not very likely.

Again, this is the importance of dealing with an agent who know what they are doing and have a lot of personal and professional experience with IULs. And let's get real for a moment. If the markets went down for four or five years in a row, your 401K would likely be in much worse shape than the IUL.

And TRIPLE ZERO™ plans also have fixed accounts (like a 1-year CD) that typically pay 3%-4.5%—even during the last recession/bear market. Instead of doing nothing, you could move all or part of your cash value out of the indexes and into this account on any policy anniversary.

And, of course, you could do a 1035 tax-free exchange to a new IUL or tax-deferred annuity if you just wanted out. But you (and I) wouldn't just do NOTHING about it.

3) Caps, Spreads, and Participation Rates could change.

This is also true. But the huge misconception here is that the insurer benefits by reducing them. Insurers use options to give you upside market potential, with the protection of a 0% floor.

The two reasons those things could happen (and likely will go both up and down) are: 1) the cost of options (the higher the market's volatility, the more options tend to cost) and 2) interest rate changes in the insurers' portfolio of bonds. They're as subject to interest rates as everyone else. We're all getting similar bond returns.

Insurers are agnostic whether you put your funds in the fixed account or in one or more of the indexes. They do not profit by lowering caps, spreads, or participation rates. With rising interest rates now, IULs are getting even better.

My clients and I have seen changes in caps in both directions over the years from the top insurers—who worry about market share and keeping agents recommending their policies instead of the competition.

Generally, the caps, etc., go up and down slowly across most IUL insurers at roughly similar time frames due to the economy as a whole, and the competitive nature of the business. No insurer wants to be left in the dust. Right now caps, spreads, and par rates are getting even better.

By the way, the "dividends" of whole life insurance policies are also affected by changes in interest rates and expenses. So are the banks. None of us are in control.

TRIPLE ZERO™ Checklist

There are some 138 IUL policies from about four dozen insurers. Before we end this discussion of TRIPLE ZERO™ plans as they relate to the Get Me to ZERO™ (another book of mine) goal, I'd like to share a checklist of what I consider to be non-negotiable features of an IUL policy—should you want to own one that will help you pay as little income taxes in retirement as possible.

#1) Financial Strength of the Insurance Company. In my opinion, the company should have an "A" rating from AM Best. An "A+" rating is even better. I also like to see the insurer have at least 10-12 years of offering IUL plans so that we can judge their history with the product. And what percentage of total life insurance sales do their IULs represent? The bigger the percentage—the better, as this shows commitment to the product.

2) Multiple Index Strategies Available. Long ago, the annual point-to-point S&P 500 index was the only strategy most TRIPLE ZERO™ plans offered. But having 3-5 indexes (S&P 500 and others) and strategies with attractive spreads and participation rates on those indexes are even better (to take advantage when markets have significant gains).

3) Loan Options. In my own TRIPLE ZERO™ policies, I have both the "wash loan" and "participating loan" options (different insurers name them differently). The guaranteed wash loan cost should be less than 0.5% and as close to 0% as possible—at least after the 6th policy year.

And the participating loan option should have a guaranteed loan rate of 5%-6%. If it "floats" with the Moody's Bond Index (or similar), the rate may be lower when interest rates are low, like 2009-2021. But I'd like it to be capped at no more than 6% (when interest rates go high).

Not only are both loan options available in all my policies, but I can freely change from one loan type to the other on any policy anniversary. That gives me great flexibility and gives me the best of both worlds.

4) The policy illustration must show both projected expenses and Internal Rates of Returns (IRRs) so these are not hidden from you. If the agent will not do this, then find another agent who will. And ask the agent what plan he/she has if the insurer raises these costs for any reason.

5) Daily or Weekly Sweeps. Premium dollars arrive at insurers every business day. The best IULs take that premium and buy options every day or at least weekly. It's less advantageous to an IUL owner to have that money sitting around for a month or quarter, waiting to get returns that are "linked" to the markets.

A daily or weekly option sweep also indicates the level of IUL premium volume an insurer gets and perhaps their long-term commitment to the IUL space.

6) Over-loan Protection. Most good IUL policies will have this today. This provision protects the policyholder from themselves. Taking too much money out of your policy through policy loans ("more" than is justified by the cash values inside your policy) can cause a policy to lapse.

Should a policy lapse (and it doesn't pay off outstanding loans and accrued interest through the death benefit), all previous distributions would be taxable. That would not be a good thing, to say the least.

The over-loan provision can protect you from this happening at all. Hopefully, you and your agent will monitor the level of distributions taken compared to policy performance—just like you would do with an IRA and all other accounts—so you don't ever run out of money.

Throughout this whole book, we've discussed using multiple strategies to pay as few taxes in retirement as possible and potentially reduce other risks like the sequence of returns risk.

I'd like to assume that readers would be just as vigilant in monitoring ALL aspects of your retirement income plan (ROTH returns, risks, expenses, etc.) on an ongoing basis.

7) Chronic Illness Provisions. As stated earlier in the book, many agents oversell the "free" LTC benefit when the TRIPLE ZERO™ plan is built, funded, and meant to provide tax-free retirement cash flow.

Depending upon when an LTC need might occur, this provision could be very valuable (if you needed it in the early policy years). It's not worth very much when the cash value and death benefit amounts are pretty similar and/or you are already taking distributions from the policy. But I would put this "free" benefit on the shopping list too!

8) Even with a TRIPLE ZERO™ plan that includes all the above unless it is properly designed and fully funded (that part is up to you), I would not buy it.

There are many ways to build an IUL. Some designs benefit the agent more than the policyholder. It's usually due to the agent not being correctly trained (or trained by a commission-driven selfish agent) that could cause this to happen. But unfortunately, sometimes it's simply an agent's plain greed.

An IUL "pro" can tell in 3 minutes of looking at any policy illustration if the agent designed the policy for his/her own benefit... or yours. It's worth a second opinion.

Some Frequently Asked Questions... Answered

What if tax rates don't go up and/or tax brackets and deductions are not changed for the worse in the next 10-30+ years?

Good question. With all of our country's unfunded obligations plus $34+ Trillion of actual debt, do you really think that tax rates, brackets, and deductions will be lowered for you in the future? If so, then these strategies, at least from a tax standpoint, won't make sense for you.

Tax rates don't have to double as David Walker suggests they must for your taking action to bear fruit. If tax rates (and other similar IRS tax levers) just move against you by 1%, then contributing to ROTHs, converting to ROTHs, 72(t)s, etc., will have been a wise tax decision.

That's on top of trying to avoid taxation on your Social Security, avoiding RMDs, plus all the other non-tax benefits described in this book. If tax rates increase by just 5%... you've hit a home run. And you can't use our special Catapult financing anywhere else but life insurance.

Can Congress change the tax laws for TRIPLE ZERO™ plans?

Yes, they can. In fact, they have done so three times during the 1980s (TAMRA, DEFRA, and TEFRA). However, in each of those cases, they grandfathered the better previous tax treatment to all existing life insurance contracts (yes—it was even better back then). Should they make changes once again, I'm betting that history will repeat itself and my own life policies will be grandfathered like before. Members of Congress own these types of life policies, too! Truth be told, they could change the rules on ROTHs, too. Congress could even eliminate the IRS and "income taxes" altogether and replace them with a huge "sales tax" on every product or service we buy. The more you spend, the more taxes you pay. Who knows?

But I believe one must plan based on the present tax laws—rather than not doing any planning at all because we don't know what a Congress and a President will do 10, 15, or 30 years from now. That's the only prudent course of action. Does that make sense to you?

Would it be beneficial to own more than one TRIPLE ZERO™ plan?

Well, that depends on many factors. I didn't start out with five policies. I bought one with what annual amount I wanted to contribute to it. Then, I was able to contribute more (but the MEC limits would not allow me to add it to the 1st policy), so I applied for my next policy. And so on. I'd like to do one more, but we'll see.

Sometimes, it makes perfect sense to have a policy or Catapult on each spouse since the other appreciates the death benefit as well as the living benefits (tax-free cash flow, the Private Reserve, potential LTC benefits, etc.).

I also have clients (including myself) who like to use more than one insurer because of the different index strategies each one offers. I like index diversification (with FIAs, too), the same as I like investment portfolio diversification. But if someone just wanted to put $500 a month into a TRIPLE ZERO™ plan, I'd suggest they use just one policy.

Are retirement plans like Traditional IRAs, ROTHs, 401Ks, and TRIPLE ZERO™ plans protected from creditors?

In this lawsuit-happy society we live in, creditor protection is important! First of all, I'm not an attorney (nor do I play one on TV). The following is my understanding. Rather than debt issues, the legal issue my clients worry about most is a civil lawsuit (teenager's driving accident, etc.). And business owners are more worried than most.

Retirement plans at work (ERISA plans like 401Ks, etc.) have the most creditor protections. Typically, the only people who can get a piece of your 401K savings while it's inside your plan at work are 1) the IRS and 2) an ex-spouse as part of a divorce decree. Other than that, the 401K creditor protection is virtually impenetrable to most creditors.

If you rollover those 401K funds to an IRA, it can start to get a little more complicated since there are two basic types of creditor protection; 1) creditor protection in bankruptcy and 2) creditor protection in any type of non-bankruptcy event (civil lawsuit)—think O.J. Simpson.

As to creditor protection in a bankruptcy, in 2005, a Federal law provided your retirement account with strong bankruptcy protection. Under that law, 401K and other ERISA plans (work-based) and pensions were given unlimited protection in bankruptcy proceedings.

And if you roll that money over to your IRA, the unlimited protection in bankruptcy proceedings will follow right along with it.

As to non-bankruptcy creditor protection scenarios (lawsuits), while the unlimited bankruptcy protection those funds had inside the 401K follows those dollars in a rollover to an IRA, the creditor protection in non-bankruptcy situations may not. It depends on where you live.

When 401K funds are rolled over to an IRA, the non-bankruptcy creditor protection will be determined by your state's laws. According to IRA expert and CPA Ed Slott, "In some states, that protection will be roughly equivalent to the protection the funds had while they were in your 401K. In other states, your protection could be much weaker."

And believe it or not, to complicate matters even more, some states actually provide traditional IRAs and Roth IRAs with different levels of creditor protection!

Contributory IRAs have federal protection in bankruptcy proceedings (limited to $1,362,800). In non-bankruptcy situations, only state law applies to both ROTHs and traditional IRAs. And the IRS can always levy your IRA, too. TRIPLE ZERO™ plans: The cash accumulation and/or death benefit in life insurance policies are partially or fully protected from most creditors and lawsuits in most states (100% creditor protected in AL, FL, KY, IL, IN, MD, MO, NC, NJ, TN, TX, and perhaps some other states).

By the way, your taxable brokerage accounts, bank accounts, real estate (many primary residences, vacation homes, and investment properties), and most other assets are <u>NOT</u> generally protected from bankruptcy, civil court judgments, and non-bankruptcy cases. The rules vary by state, so please consult an attorney.

Although an "umbrella" insurance policy will not protect you against any creditor issues, it will help protect your assets from lawsuits due to and arising from (and above and beyond) your car and homeowner's insurance limits. I always recommend you get at least $1 million of umbrella coverage. I have a $2 million umbrella policy but should probably increase that to $3-4 million. A to-do 2024!

What if I'm not healthy enough to even qualify for any life insurance? (You get turned down or are very highly rated).

That happens more than most people think. When this occurs, we use a "surrogate" insured. You would be the policy owner, control all the cash accumulation, designate the beneficiaries, etc. But the death benefit would be paid on someone else's passing away.

There must be some insurable interest (a real reason to do this) in order for you to own a policy on another person's life. Typically, this would be a spouse, child, parent, or business partner.

I can buy stocks, bonds, and mutual funds on my own. Why would I need an insurance agent (who gets a commission) to own a TRIPLE ZERO™ plan?

You can buy term life insurance online (although you typically still must take some type of health exam if the policy's death benefit is over $100,000). Even though that's simple to do, you do not avoid a commission being paid. The owner of the website must be a licensed agent and is selling the same exact policies as the guy sitting at your kitchen table. The policies online are exactly the same as those from an agent. A commission gets paid in either case.

The consumer does not save a dime by foregoing a live person's help and advice. To my knowledge, there is no way to buy an IUL online. Perhaps there is or will be at some point. But as you probably understand after reading this book, there is a lot more to designing and positioning this product than just saying you want a million-dollar, 20-year term policy and want to know the monthly premium. And especially so with Catapult plans.

Even most insurance agents don't have a clue about IULs. And if (when?) you can buy an IUL online, just like with any other insurance policy (car, renters, home, etc.), a commission will be paid to the owner of the website (who must be a licensed agent in the state you reside in).

The commission does not add to your premium, so I see no benefit to not getting the most experienced, hands-on professional help you can for the same exact premium dollars contributed.

What if I really like the attributes of a TRIPLE ZERO™ plan, but I can't afford to contribute much more than to my ROTH right now?

Great job on contributing to a ROTH! You have begun the journey to TAX-FREE. Do you have a ROTH 401K option too? Many times, I can help folks "find the money" to start your IUL now. There are four major "money moves" we use to be more efficient in your financial life and fund a sizable TRIPLE ZERO™—<u>without</u> changing your lifestyle.

But if not, if you can afford to invest at least $500/month to a TRIPLE ZERO™ plan within 3, 5, or 10 years (depending upon your age, sex, and health), you might consider getting a "convertible term" policy until you can afford your IUL. A convertible term policy gives you immediate death benefit coverage and locks in your insurability to upgrade to an IUL within a certain number of years (sometimes up to 30 yrs).

Some insurers will even give you some credit on your previously paid term premiums. But, the convertible term policy will typically only allow you to convert to an IUL product from that same insurance company. So, you want to make sure that you buy the term insurance from a company that you want to own eventually your IUL.

Mark, my husband, and I make over $850,000 a year in our construction business. Doesn't it make sense for us to take every deduction we can get today?

There are many factors to consider. You are currently in the highest tax bracket with marginal rates of 37% plus a 3.8% surtax on any investment income from taxable accounts. Historically, those in the highest tax brackets will remain in the highest brackets (the rich get richer). In 2026, the top tax rate is set to go back to 39.7%. I expect it will go higher.

The top 1% of earners pay 39% of <u>total</u> personal income taxes! The top 10% pay 70%. The bottom 50% pay only 3%.

If you think your taxes in retirement will be lower, then take your full deductions in the traditional 401K now. If not, and a ROTH 401K option is available to you, I'd do that. In either case, hopefully, you are saving a ton of money outside of your qualified 401k plans for your future. In a taxable account, you'll get 1099s and pay taxes every year. Paying taxes on earnings you aren't even spending. There's the perfect place for a TRIPLE ZERO™. Unlimited contributions, no income restrictions, no 1099s and tax-free access (Private Reserve), and retirement cash flow with no market risk. Perhaps even the Catapult plan. I'd need more info regarding your situation and goals.

And finally, why hasn't my CPA told me about IULs?

Good question. There are almost as many reasons for that as there are CPAs, Enrolled Agents (EAs), and other tax professionals.

First of all, in my experience, I've found that most CPAs were never trained on cash value life insurance (nor annuities, for that matter). I've recently hosted another 4-hour Continuing Education class (CPE credits) for CPAs on these subjects. Based on their past course evaluations, they love it. The difference in their knowledge of this subject from the beginning of the class... to the end is like "night and day."

And we've only scratched the surface of these two subjects in four hours. Let alone teaching other advanced financial planning such as Social Security strategies, ROTH, 72(t)s, QCDs, reverse mortgages, Catapults, Private Reserve, etc.

I could not charge somebody to do tax returns after taking a 4-hour course. We each have our areas of expertise. I've also found many CPAs are simply overwhelmed with their primary duties of tax preparation, audits, and compliance paperwork—especially during tax season. Many of these dedicated tax pros are working 12-15-hour days, 6 or 7 days a week during peak tax season.

In most cases, you only pay them to produce timely and accurate tax returns <u>based only on the information you provided</u>—not for proactive tax planning.

While they all are experts at recording tax history, many view their job as saving you taxes today—rather than preparing you for the potential of higher future taxes, avoiding RMDs, taxation of SS, etc. Most folks want instant gratification. Clients say, "Save me taxes TODAY!"

Few CPAs are compensated by you to provide longer-term proactive tax planning. Many would like to do this and provide more extensive planning services for those clients who could benefit.

One of my 2024 business initiatives is helping CPAs "shine" by extending their relationship with their clients through a much deeper dive into their present financial circumstances and future goals with comprehensive financial and tax planning. I'll even use outside specialists when appropriate.

To accomplish this initiative, I'm affiliated with two groups that help CPAs change their practice. To do more of the work they like to do and find most interesting (planning and advice) and perhaps less of the more mundane functions someone else in the office could do.

For example, our CPA Team-Based Model is a solution-focused planning platform to empower CPAs to proactively increase their value to their clients with comprehensive financial, business, and tax advice.

Holistic strategies and solutions based on the client's goals with the CPA and advisor working together on an encompassing plan to strategically meet them.

The CPA and advisor are working for a win-win-win for their top clients. The client gets much more proactive and advanced planning, the CPA gets more interesting tax work (overall wealth management oversight), and is compensated for it, and the advisor earns a new long-term and happy client.

And this team-based planning would typically go far beyond the TRIPLE ZERO™ strategy. There's much planning that can be done to make their financial life better—particularly for successful business owners and the affluent. But EVERYONE can benefit from being more proactive!

And frankly, CPAs are no different from other professionals (dentists, CEOs, homebuilders, doctors, lawyers, FBI agents, coders, contractors, financial advisors, etc.). There is a wide range of skills, experience, passion, and results.

So yes, more CPAs will "get it" and recommend this planning for people who are concerned about rising tax rates, lower brackets, and fewer legal deductions.

What's Next?

Hopefully, you have fully read and understood this book about TRIPLE ZERO™ plans and like what you've learned so far. Hopefully, you'll want to explore these plans for YOU!

How about seeing if a Catapult plan would work for you? You get 3:1 leverage at low interest rates and effectively no cap on contributions. No loan applications. No guarantees. No loan documents. No out-of-pocket interest or principal payments. Not even a signature on a loan. Unbeatable.

Can you even imagine the future tax-free income you could enjoy by "stacking" Catapult plans? By stacking, I mean once you have funded your five years of contributions, you start another Catapult plan and then another. Wow.

When markets have big drops, do you like the "ZERO is your Hero" protection? How about the "Lock-in" mechanism protecting all past gains? Or the index "reset" that takes advantage of bear markets with a fresh start?

With the lock-in and reset, you never need to get back to even before you make new gains. An S&P 500 index fund doesn't work that way. Nor do most other investments.

Do you like the fact that you are not limited by any IRS regulations on how much you can contribute a year? There are effectively no annual limits to moving funds from ever-taxable accounts to the forever TAX-FREE zone.

Nor are there any income limits—so even those with extremely high incomes can participate! Just envisage $100K or 250K premiums (5 yrs. only) into a Catapult plan.

Even without financing (no bank loans), the Private Reserve strategy is also a big deal. You cannot use any IRA to have your savings earn money in two places at once. What another game-changer this strategy could be.

Should a TRIPLE ZERO™ plan play a role in YOUR retirement planning? Will it add value both before and during your retirement? What if taxes skyrocket? What about a market crash? Why not contact me today to see how a TRIPLE ZERO™ plan might look for you? There's <u>no cost nor any obligation</u> to explore how these plans might work for you.

You can contact me by phone at 770-777-8309 (office) or by email: mark@SmartFinancialPlanning.com

Let's book a quick 20 or 30-minute introductory call.

My "WHY": "To help people proactively maximize every one of their financial resources and opportunities so they can enjoy a much fuller life and make a positive impact on our world." TRIPLE ZERO™ plans give you that opportunity.

You see, I'm sick and tired of advisors, the media, the internet, etc., only giving half of the story to slant whatever their agenda is. For example, your 401K plan advisor wants you to put in as much as possible and "sells" you on the big tax-deduction today—but not the future tax cost you'll pay.

And quite frankly, I'd also like to introduce you to my services and other strategies. I'm not your traditional CFP®. Never have been. My planning is "outside the box" and always has been. Our team has so many strategies to help our clients reach their financial goals with more certainty and predictability. For example, I can help many business owners SAVE TAXES today with other advanced strategies.

You probably surmise that I really like IULs (I own 5 of them and Norma has two), so you are correct. But that doesn't mean a TRIPLE ZERO™ plan is the right option for you! And our fast-growing investment firm helps clients improve traditional, ROTH IRAs and old 401K improve results.

Our national firm manages $8 BILLION of assets at Fidelity and Schwab. Our firm was listed three times on Inc. Magazine's 500 Fastest-Growing Companies.

Each portfolio is personalized to the investor based on what's important to them: growth, income, etc. With daily oversight from our investment committee, our clients know that their investments are never neglected.

And I help many of my clients with other financial and tax planning services. Comprehensive, holistic planning with less risk/lower lifetime taxes are our group's mantras.

I spend about $20,000 a year traveling to attend non-traditional financial conferences, classes, and training to be a better advisor for my clients. For example, Tom Wheelwright is Robert Kiyosaki's (Rich Dad, Poor Dad) personal CPA. I convinced him to let me attend his 3-day, high-end, for-CPAs-only training. I was the only non-CPA in the room, and I taught a number of them about Catapult and Private Reserve. None of them knew these strategies even existed. Not one CPA in the class!

So, I can help you in many areas of your financial life too!

But let me give one final thought on TRIPLE ZERO™ and especially Catapult plans. There truly is nothing like this opportunity out there—especially in the TAX-FREE world. Let's invest 20 minutes on the phone to see if there may be a fit for you and your financial and retirement goals.

About the Author: Mark J. Orr, CFP® RICP®
PROACTIVE Tax Planning, LLC
www.SmartFinancialPlanning.com
770-777-8309 Office
mark@SmartFinancialPlanning.com

Mark has been a practicing Certified Financial Planner™ since 2000. Certified Financial Planners are held to the strictest ethical and fiduciary standards. He has also earned the year-long Retirement Income Certified Professional® (RICP®) designation. Since 1997, he has held life, health, and the Series 7 Securities license (no longer carried) and became a Registered Investment Advisor soon thereafter, owning his own fee-based firm from 1999-2016.

He is now an Investment Advisor Representative with Retirement Wealth Advisors, where Brookstone Capital/RWA manages his clients' stock and bond market-based investments, applying tactical money management mainly using index ETFs. These fee-only accounts are allocated into portfolios based on a client's risk tolerance, tax situation, time horizon, and income and legacy goals. Mark always acts in his role as a fiduciary.

Our first focus is on reducing sequence of returns risk (and drawdown) while capturing as much of the market's upside as possible with daily oversight from our full-time professional investment committee.

He is also the author of three other books: 1) "Social Security Income Planning: The Baby Boomers' 2024 Guide to Maximize Your Retirement Benefits" 2) "I Didn't Know Annuities Could Do That!" 3) "Get Me to Zero: Use the Tax Code to Pay as Little as ZERO Taxes During Retirement" (which includes much of this book fully describing the TRIPLE ZERO™ plan as one of the seven planning strategies) as well as several white papers and eBooks

He has led dozens of public seminars on various financial planning and retirement topics. He's been quoted twice in both USA TODAY and cnbc.com as well as being a guest on several morning radio shows across the country.

Prior to the financial services business, Mark spent the early part of his career in the luxury resort real estate development and marketing industry—managing $100 million of sales in Europe over a 7-year period. That was back when that was "real" money —lol! After that, he owned a few franchises and then sold those businesses.

He is a four-time past board member of his Rotary Club and continues to be active in community service through the Rotary Club. On a personal note, Mark and Norma live in Alpharetta, Georgia, and love to travel—especially to warm sandy beaches. Staying in good shape is very important to him and he enjoys great red wine.

Finally, he is the very proud father of three grown children (Megan, Marina, and Michael) and two wonderful grandchildren.

Acknowledgments and Disclosures

The opinions and views written in this book are those of the author and do not necessarily represent those of any person, organization, or firm that I have been associated with (either in the past, are currently, or may be in the future). This book is intended to provide general information only, and that no individual professional financial advice is offered herein. The author is not a CPA or certified tax professional. The author is not an attorney.

Neither the author nor publisher intend to or is rendering any professional services including, but not limited to: tax advice, investment advice, insurance advice, legal advice, or mortgage advice. This book, nor any words written within its pages, should be interpreted as giving any such personal/individual advice and should not be relied upon.

Any mention of financial products, investment managers, investment advisory services, etc., should not be construed as an offer to buy, sell, or exchange any financial product or service.

The author and publisher absolutely disclaim any responsibility for any reader taking any liability, loss incurred as a consequence of any implementation (or even non-implementation) on the information provided herein. No book intended as general information and sold to the general public can be construed to offer specific and personal financial, investment, insurance, tax, or legal advice.

All readers who require personal advice and professional financial service should seek an experienced, qualified, and appropriately licensed advisor (relevant to such advice) and not solely rely on the contents of this or any book to make any personal financial decision.

Insurance products are not investments. All insurance products are backed based solely on the financial strength and the claims-paying ability of the insurer that issues the policy or contract. Use of the terms "Principal Protected," "Guaranteed," "Safe," "Secure" and any and all such similar words when describing any insurance product is based entirely on the fact of contractual guarantees, which rely on the financial strength and claims-paying ability of the insurance company.

Index Universal Life (IUL) and Fixed Indexed Annuity (FIA) insurance policies are not stock, bond, or investments and have no direct participation in the stock or bond markets. You are not buying any bonds, shares of stocks, or shares in an index, nor do they include dividends or interest of any stock, bond, or market index.

Investment Advisory Services are offered through Retirement Wealth Advisors, (RWA), an SEC Registered Investment Advisor.

Mark J. Orr and Brookstone Capital Mgmt/RWA are not affiliated. Investing involves risk, including the potential loss of principal. No investment strategy can guarantee a profit or protect against loss in periods of declining values. Opinions expressed are subject to change without notice and are not intended as investment advice or to predict future performance.

Past performance does not guarantee future results. All life insurance, fixed annuity products, and fees for advanced income tax planning for business owners are sold separately through Mark J. ORR, CFP®/PROACTIVE Tax Planning LLC.

Again, contact me directly should you want to explore how a CATAPULT or TRIPLE ZERO™ plan can dramatically improve your financial life—both now and in the future.

With or without the PRIVATE RESERVE or CATAPULT strategies, you can truly transform your retirement lifestyle by sending less of your income to the IRS—keeping more for yourself! It's your retirement, and you can do better.

And you don't have to wait to benefit from TRIPLE ZERO™ plans until retirement since you can access most of the cash for any reason at all—without penalty, plus having the protection of the death benefit along the way.

SMART
FINANCIAL PLANNING

Made in the USA
Coppell, TX
13 February 2025